COLLABRO

Our Story

COLLABRO

Our Story

BLINK

bringing you closer

Published by Blink Publishing
107-109 The Plaza,
535 Kings Road,
Chelsea Harbour,
London, SW10 0SZ

www.blinkpublishing.co.uk
facebook.com/blinkpublishing
twitter.com/blinkpublishing

978 1905 825 790

A CIP catalogue of this book is available from the British Library.

Design by www.envydesign.co.uk

Printed and bound by Clays Ltd, St Ives Plc

1 3 5 7 9 10 8 6 4 2

Papers used by Blink Publishing are natural, recyclable products made from
wood grown in sustainable forests. The manufacturing processes conform to the
environmental regulations of the country of origin.

Blink Publishing is an imprint of the Bonnier Publishing Group

www.bonnierpublishing.co.uk

CONTENTS

INTRODUCTION

From the moment we all met up above a little pub in south London and sang together for the very first time, this group has felt special. As you are about to read, we were standing in a tiny upstairs room above a bar and sang 'Bring Him Home' together, Collabro's first ever song as a five-piece. At that exact moment, we all just looked at each other – it felt like a really important event in all of our lives. There was something exciting going on, something magical. It was one of those moments that we will never forget.

Of course, we have been so lucky to experience many more incredible moments since that very first song together: early performances, TV auditions, winning *Britain's Got Talent*, film premieres, record signings, massive festival gigs, our album release, West End curtain calls and all the crazy experiences that Collabro has created for us in between. We have tried to capture those moments in this book, and hopefully you will feel the same sense of emotion, the same incredible feelings of excitement, tension, happiness, nerves, jubilation and pride that we have experienced along the way.

We've also tried to tell you a little bit about our lives before we even knew each other. We may have been five separate people growing up with a common dream, but our struggles to break through and make something of our love for musical theatre eventually drew us together into one place at the same time.

In that room above a pub in south London.

That's when it all finally came together and this unbelievable journey began.

Since that moment, it's been the most amazing ride of our lives.

None of this would have been possible without your support. By reading about our lives before Collabro, as well as our thoughts and feelings since the group has taken off, we hope that you feel as if you have been there right by our side for every step of the way. We have so much more to achieve, to strive for, to share with you, so hopefully you will be there with us for many more incredible moments to come.

PART ONE

CHAPTER 1

JAMIE

I feel very lucky that Collabro has enjoyed the success it has had so far. However, even as a kid I was very lucky, I've had a lovely family life. Honestly, I can't tell you, my mum and dad are the best parents ever. I know everyone says that but they are the best parents in the world. I adore them both and we are the best of friends.

My absolute idol in my life is my mum, always will be. She came from nothing. Her family travelled a lot because her dad was in the Army, in fact before Mum was even born they lived as far afield as Africa. The family eventually moved back to Halifax in northern England but when my mum was just three years old, her dad left. A new man called Albert later came into the family home and Mum always saw him as her real dad. Even when Albert came along and became their dad, they still had very little money. It was mushrooms and butter on toast as a treat and they would go to school wearing clothes that had been passed down. They were a very poor family.

Despite her difficult upbringing and very much against the odds, she worked incredibly hard and won a scholarship to a grammar school, then went to study English at Newcastle University. She was the youngest female chief executive of an NHS trust to be appointed at that time and she was also nominated as one of the 50 most inspirational women in the NHS for a book published to celebrate the health service's 50th birthday. I am so proud of her.

The lack of money that Mum had in her childhood has created in her an immense drive to do well, to make her life better and to make her children's lives better than she had experienced. That's not any kind of detrimental comment on her own mum's amazing efforts, it's just a fact that their life was very tough. You always have a special connection with someone in your life and with me it is my mum. She's a very wise woman but she is also incredibly strong, independent and very beautiful. You can only describe her as that and I can only hope to be like her one day. She has influenced me in so many ways. Mum used to sing to me, she has a beautiful voice and plays guitar. I get my love of reading from her, too. She would tell me about books such as *Tess of the d'Urbervilles*, *The Mayor of Casterbridge*, all these wonderful stories. She encouraged me to read – I ploughed through *The Hobbit* when I was barely into primary school. She is a force of nature, that's what she is.

Fast-forward to Collabro and as I am writing this chapter I've just got a card through the door from Mum. That's no surprise because I still get a card from her every week. We speak on the phone every day but she still writes to me every week. Even now, she signs off all her letters to me with *carpe diem*, 'seize the day'. Sometimes she even sends me £20, which evidently I don't need but she will say, 'Go and get yourself a drink on me, Jamie.' What an amazing woman.

Mine is a family of strong women. Her mum, my nana, was

massively important in terms of me getting into singing. Nana was a proudly working-class Yorkshire woman, from a Yorkshire mill town, who had the most incredibly difficult life. She was one of 17 children, only 11 of whom survived into adulthood. She came from a family of strong women and when her husband left and she had to bring up Mum and her two older sisters as a single parent, she just went out and got two jobs and got on with it. She was a cleaner in a hospital and also became a nurse when the National Health Service first started.

For some amazing reason, Nana just adored opera, even though she couldn't even understand the words of the songs. She just used to *love* opera more than anything else. Musical theatre too. I think it was probably pure escapism. That is what those genres offer to so many people, that sense of escapism. She just loved those styles of music with a passion.

When Andrea Bocelli first broke through into the wider public's awareness, Nana used to play his album all the time. She was already listening to Pavarotti and Lesley Garrett but Bocelli was her favourite. His 1997 album *Romanza* was a landmark in the world of crossover because everyone bought it and the track 'Time To Say Goodbye' was, for me, the song of the 1990s. I adore him; I think he has the most phenomenal voice. It is entirely because of my nana that I knew of him when I was so young. I distinctly remember the day when my nana first brought out his record. I was in her front room, she had this dog called Sable and I was lying on a sofa using the dog as a pillow when suddenly this man's voice came on the stereo – there was just something so warm about the sound, something so emotional, so incredible. Even though I was relatively young, only eight at the time, that album stopped me dead in my tracks.

Later in life I would train in opera and become a vocal coach, so I would come to understand why Bocelli is such a phenomenal singer. Of course, back then I knew none of that, I was just reacting to his voice on an emotional level as a young kid. For me, that is what music should always be about, listening to songs that make a connection with you. That album did that for me and 'Time To Say Goodbye' was the song that set me on the path to being in Collabro. My nana was a huge influence on me in terms of my music and also just in my life. I adored her but sadly she died when I was only 11. I would also like to make a special mention of my Grandma Jenny, my dad's mum, who was inspirational – a cuddly, kind, baking grandma who was the matriarch of the family. She died when I was 19, and I sang 'Time To Say Goodbye' at her funeral. She was a wonderful, sweet, kind woman.

I was distraught when I lost my nana. I had a lovely childhood, but there were difficult times because my family had a lot of loss and I really felt that when I was so young. Most people have their grandparents until they are at least in their mid-20s, but I lost three of my grandparents way before that; my surviving grandad is currently in the later stages of Alzheimer's. I lost an uncle I was close to, as well. In some ways that sounds quite turbulent and difficult but do you know what? I never felt anything other than totally loved and looked after to the ends of the earth. That is an amazing feeling to be able to savour. How lucky am I?

I have a sister, Caytee, who is two years younger than me. She is my absolute world and my best friend. We are very close and I am so proud of her. She is incredibly intelligent and is going to have the most amazing career as a doctor. She is such a lovely, kind, and thoughtful person. Beautiful too.

My interest in performing music actually started before I heard

Bocelli, because I started playing the cello in Year Three, which I enjoyed and was quite good at – I got to Grade 7. Mum always encouraged me to connect with the music. I used to play for Mum and she would say, 'Right, that was technically very good, Jamie, but you didn't feel *moved*.' She would make me do it again until I *felt* the music. She called it 'feeling the music'. I have tried to hold on to that idea throughout my career, so even if I can sing a piece technically well, there still has to be that connection. That's entirely down to my mum.

My primary school years were very happy. I went to a very small village school called Rickleton Primary. I loved it – the teachers were great. I had nice friends and I would come home and play with my sister straight after school. I felt safe, happy and loved. The school did a few musicals and plays, the usual primary school stuff like *Oliver!* and I was involved, but at this stage it was just because all the kids were. I enjoyed it but there weren't any leading roles or solos yet. I loved my primary school years though – they were some of the happiest times of my life.

One really fun early singing experience I had was appearing on the TV as part of a group performing a charity single. The song raised funds for various kids' charities and the well-known TV agony aunt Denise Robertson was involved. That was fun. At school I was always very involved with the orchestra too. I just loved school – all the different lessons – I never got bored. It was nice to learn so I was very attentive, especially in English literature and music.

When I was 11 I was diagnosed with dyspraxia. I have a fairly mild strain of the disorder which mainly affects my hand-eye co-ordination, but also sequencing. I was born two months prematurely with severe jaundice and was very poorly. I was in an incubator for two weeks before Mum could even hold me. As a consequence I had very minor brain damage, but this wasn't diagnosed until quite late in primary school because I did well at everything. In later life this would manifest itself as mild dyspraxia. I used to drop things all the time at school and be ridiculed for that. It didn't impact massively on my school life but there were times when it made my days harder than I would have liked, particularly in class or around other kids. (The interesting thing is that I have never had problems with sequencing words and music though.)

My parents separated when I was 13. I know a lot of children find that very difficult but I think, looking back, it was definitely for the best. I don't know why but I felt quite emotionally aware at that age. My sister found it harder because she was three years younger than me. I had gone to senior school, I was choosing my exams and so I was also old enough to realise that something wasn't quite right. They weren't as happy when they were married as they are now. My dad has found someone new, Norma, and she is amazing, like a second mum. Of course, there is always that transition period, where we were thinking, *Who is this person?* For a teenager and his younger sister to have someone new in their lives is really challenging, but to be fair I would imagine it was pretty terrifying for her as well, because she never had kids. It took about a year and a half and then suddenly everything fell into place. My dad is amazing because after I told him I was gay he just never treated me differently at all. He has always accepted all of my partners and treated them like his own and Norma is the same. They're genuinely lovely people and both retired now, so they live part of the year abroad, and it gives me so much joy to see that they have found happiness together. I love to go over to Dad and Norma's house now and they both cook amazing food, and I definitely got my love of red wine from him! It's really nice that they have never lived far from my home and that I have always had easy access to them, as I value both of them very much and they are a big part of my life. They have always supported my singing and been in the audience for everything and they teamed up with my mum and sister to campaign for us throughout *Britain's Got Talent*, which was really special for me to see. When parents separate, the children can sometimes feel as if they have lost their relationship with one parent – for me and my sister that was never the case. In fact, we feel like we gained a family member, because with Norma it is as if she has always been there. She is an amazing woman.

Back when my parents were separating, one of the spare bedrooms had a TV with a video player built in. I would always sneak in there and pop a video of *Les Misérables* in and watch it over and over again. I think I must've watched the tenth anniversary video of that musical about 100 times (as well as seeing the actual show maybe ten times!).

For my secondary school years I went to the Dame Allan's school in Newcastle, which at the time was a private school for boys. At first I was quite intimidated by the size of the building and the sheer number of kids compared to my tiny primary school, but I soon got used to that and quickly made some great friends. I have mostly wonderful memories of my time there.

Singing for me really started around the age of 13 when my voice broke at secondary school. One of the school shows featured a medley of *Les Misérables* and I auditioned and got to sing 'Empty Chairs At Empty Tables' which is a solo by Marius Pontmercy. That's rather ironic because now as an adult, I would never get that part – I am too tall and big, Marius needs to be more weedy! That was my first ever solo, a big turning point for me. At the time most people didn't know that I sang and they certainly didn't expect this big bass operatic voice to come out of this 13-year-old boy. My mum video-taped the performance and it's really fun to watch back – people were really shocked. Perhaps not surprisingly, I tried to sing like Andrea Bocelli at the time, only lower, so the audience was really taken aback.

That first solo performance was the start for me. I started joining amateur dramatic productions whenever I could. Quite soon after, I landed the role of Marius in a production by Talent, a local youth amateur dramatics company. I can honestly say that was the best four months of my life up to that point. It was a really nice cast and it was the first time that I discovered what it felt like to be on stage in a role. I was not a particularly good actor at that point, but I can vividly remember the feeling of walking out on to the stage playing this character. I realise now that it was the same feeling that my nana loved – escapism. Something came over me and I knew there and then – I know that sounds a bit dramatic but it's true – that I wanted to be a professional singer. I really wanted to learn so I had a few singing lessons and wanted to improve. I was eager to just get better and better.

When I was 14 and working towards my GCSEs I went to Kenya for ten days on a school trip. My mum was so keen for me to experience Africa that she paid for me to go, which was so lucky. That trip was incredibly important in my young life because we sang with these kids and it was fascinating to see such a different way of life.

By this age, I knew I was gay. I didn't know anyone else who was gay so that was difficult. I was just finding out who I was. I wasn't unpopular at school, I had loads of close friends, that was a blessing, but I wasn't one of the cool crowd or the sporty bunch.

JAMIE

Around this time I also started to play the pubs, working men's clubs and smaller theatres around the north-east, trying to build up a little bit of a following for my singing. I was only 14 when I started so that in itself was unusual. Some of the venues were tiny and the roughest of the rough, so it was often a hard crowd to please but I loved every minute. I was only a kid; I was overweight and really well built, about four stone heavier than I am as an adult. I had bad acne, long hair and not an awful amount of confidence.

Mum was my manager, she got all the gigs booked and my sister did the sound. I saved up to buy a little PA speaker system and we used to travel around various venues, singing to tiny crowds, big crowds, all sorts!

I think most crowds just assumed I was going to do bad rock tribute songs so when I opened up with 'Strangers In Paradise' it was always a shock. I loved going on stage in front of people who thought I wasn't going to do very well and then shocking them. I got the biggest buzz out of that.

Generally the gigs went down really well. That's not me blowing my own trumpet, I just think the nature of the music I was singing – mostly musical theatre – provoked a reaction. People can relate to the words and the story that you are telling. I always tried my best to make an emotional connection with the music and hope that the crowds picked up on that. It was a really special time in my life because I was just discovering what songs worked for me, whether that was pop, musical theatre, opera, swing or a mixture of all of them.

At the time there were two other people floating around the scene – Joe McElderry and Jade from Little Mix. Joe was a good lad and Jade is just the nicest girl – I always thought she was like South Shields' own Diana Ross.

Normally if it was a quiet evening there might only be 20 people in a small club. There were even times when I sang to virtually empty rooms. However, I also did some festivals in front of 5,000 people. You have to just do your best with whoever and whatever is put in front of you – don't complain, just get on with it. They have paid their money and deserve a show. There were times when I was treated pretty badly; I was just the hired entertainment so I didn't get food or drinks, I didn't even get paid that much. I was just shoved on stage, did my performance and went home. Some of the crowds and venue owners could be pretty dismissive, but there were also a lot of lovely people on that circuit. I have no complaints; I loved every minute and learnt so much.

When I was 16 I enrolled for a project called World Challenge. The idea was that you raised money to travel to Africa to contribute to communities that needed help. My team, for instance, went there to renovate an orphanage. I was just so excited to be doing something so worthwhile. I had to raise about £5,000 and with my mum I started a campaign called 'Voice Over Africa'. Everyone who sponsored me had to guess how many people I could sing in front of within a two-year period and they would give me a certain amount of money per 50 people. Initially my sponsors were saying maybe 5,000, but in fact I ended up singing in front of over 28,000! I had performed for the Freemasons before and they helped enormously, plus David Miliband, who was the MP for South Shields, occasionally booked me. I sang at various Freemason lodges, even the main one down in London. So although I was still very young, I sang at numerous formal functions in front of people such as Tony Blair, Andrew Lloyd Webber and Ken Livingstone. I was gigging constantly, clubs, pubs, anywhere I could work. Looking back I can see that I was really driven for a teenager, but at the time I didn't look at it like that, I just loved performing.

I quickly raised the money I needed so I headed off to Tanzania which, unbeknown to me, would become quite a turning point in my life. I was finding school a bit difficult at times. Like I said, I didn't know anyone else who was gay and there were all these really sporty lads around. It was an all-boys school and very much a traditional rugby institution, so that brought certain pressures. You are at an age where it is very secretive – I was only a teenager, my hormones were everywhere, and I was just not myself at all. My studies were all right but I was feeling down a lot of the time. Mum and Dad were very worried about me; I was very depressed and had genuine self-confidence problems.

Tanzania was a whole month away from my family, there were no home comforts, no Mum to back me up, none of that family strength and familiarity that I relied on. I was all on my own.

We had to climb Kilimanjaro as part of the trip but before the actual trek itself, we had to go on a so-called 'acclimatisation hike' up a smaller mountain. However, I didn't make it, I couldn't breathe properly and had to give up. I was really dejected when I didn't finish the trek. I was so depressed; I felt like I had let everyone down, I felt bad about myself, and I didn't know if they would even let me try to climb Kilimanjaro. It was a really bad moment. Coming down from that mountain during the acclimatisation trek, I just remember feeling at my absolute lowest. I was stressed about not getting up the mountain. I was stressed about having to work in a team – I wasn't used to that before, I was used to being a solo singer who ran my own life. It was just this thing about having to work with people I didn't choose to work with. I was really, really low.

Luckily, they said I could have a go at Kilimanjaro and I just said to myself, *You are going to do this, do not give up, you have to do this.* And do you know what? I was the first person to the top. I was so focused on not failing again. After that, literally as I walked back down, I felt a change in myself. From then on, that trip was a big turning point. I lost loads of weight from all the exercise, my skin cleared up from all the fresh air and sunshine, I just started to feel like a different person.

I'd been worried about having to work in a team yet I loved every one of them by the end. Of all the amazing things we did when we were out there, working with the team for five weeks was my proudest achievement. At the end of the trip, they handed out all these cards and we had to write down things like, 'Most Funny' or 'Most Clumsy' and most of my cards said, 'Most Transformed'. I came home and cut my long hair, I embraced my sexuality and I genuinely felt like a revitalised person.

Before I had gone there, I was so upset with myself all the time that I wasn't able to talk to people properly. I had lost a lot of the vivaciousness that was in my character. I was very grumpy, people couldn't chat to me and I would lose my temper easily. What Tanzania did was bring out my good qualities – I was more patient, more calm and just *happier*. I finally felt good about myself. I never came out as gay as such (I will come to that later in the book), I just sort of embraced who I was and that included focusing on the fact that I wanted to have a future in singing. So I lost some more weight, I went on this drug for reducing acne, I got my Grade 8 at singing, and really got myself sorted. I just really focused.

After Tanzania I had a period when I really enjoyed myself. I'd done well in my GCSEs and A Levels too, studying at sixth form at the same school. I had never been the academic one, my sister had always been the straight 'A' student. I was very good at certain things such as languages (especially Spanish) but I was terrible at maths!

I enjoyed sixth form. I had a nice group of friends and we had our little gang. I started driving; I was working at a pub so I had some money coming in from that and various performances. I was working really hard and paying my own way. I became a happy person.

I really loved languages so I applied to university and my thinking was to get a back-up plan, just in case the singing career didn't happen. I thought, *I will join all these university musical societies, get loads of experience then when I leave at 21 I will be at the right stage then with my voice* (because men's voices tend to sell to the industry better when they are older). Singing was absolutely the top priority. That ambition was always at the forefront of my mind but I felt like I needed a back-up plan and thank God I had it. So I went to study Spanish in Glasgow.

It was my first time away from home so, like a lot of students, I was suddenly running my own life and I'd got bills and responsibilities and needed to work out how to live on my own. Unfortunately, although after Tanzania I had really started to blossom, when I got to Glasgow it was a massive step backwards. Looking back, I wasn't really ready to move away. I didn't like my course. I didn't easily make friends because that whole Freshers vibe of going out and getting drunk all the time just didn't appeal to me. I'm not a clubber – don't get me wrong, I love bars and pubs where you can talk to your friends – but I don't go out to clubs. I hated the feeling of being hung over. So I guess that isolated me a little. I also didn't like where I was living in this awful student hall, this terrible breeze block building that felt like a prison. I had my own room and a sink, so I could just chill out on my own, but I started to feel down almost as soon as I moved in. I suffer from the winter blues terribly and that, plus the rain, didn't help. I actually love winter, it is a beautiful season but I always just feel like I want to go and hibernate. So I decked my whole room out with a massive sheepskin rug and a potted palm tree; I had mood lighting and blankets everywhere.

Unfortunately, my self-esteem was collapsing again and I'm afraid to say that while I was at Glasgow I developed an eating disorder. I had spent years being overweight and although I was now slimmer, the unhelpful feelings and lack of self-esteem had never fully left me. It had started off in a positive way, I'd come back from Tanzania and lost all that weight, but during my A Levels I just kept on going, carried on dieting. I didn't need to diet anymore but that was irrelevant. I was told that I had body dysmorphia. All I would eat was lettuce and runner beans, maybe a few pulses. I ate just enough to live off but it wasn't at all healthy.

It's a very complex illness so I can't really pinpoint any particular main reason for spiralling down this way. I think it was a combination of a few things. I was never happy with how I looked. I suffered from a lot of anxiety. The dyspraxia didn't help because obviously there are consequences of that and around other people that would make me more on edge. With the dyspraxia too, routine helps but moving away from home had stopped everything I was familiar with. That, combined with my self-esteem issues, sent me into this self-destructive cycle of not eating healthily. At one point I was ten stone which, bearing in mind I am 6' 3", is tiny. I felt a lot of shame during that particular year. I just wasn't happy in Glasgow, not happy at all.

Worse still, I stopped singing. Now I am older, I can see that this was the very worst thing I could've done when I was already feeling down. As an adult, I am very aware of how singing is absolutely crucial to my wellbeing. No matter how down I might be on a particular day, or whatever problems I am experiencing, without fail every time I get up on stage I become completely comfortable in my own skin. Performing draws out the best qualities in me. That is why I really need to perform. Back in Glasgow, I didn't yet realise this. I was just a young man struggling with life. I don't know if my unhappiness stopped me singing or stopping singing contributed to my unhappiness. All I know is that I wasn't well and I wasn't happy.

So Glasgow was a massive knockback for me. Mum and Dad were very concerned, as any parents would be. Looking back, I should've joined the musical theatre society, because then I would have met like-minded people and I would've been singing. I didn't have a group of friends; I didn't even really get a circle of friends on Facebook, which was kicking off at the time. Basically I didn't do anything for a year. Eating disorders take the life out of you. I looked like a shadow of myself.

Luckily, something in me knew that I needed to move. I knew I had to change what I was doing otherwise who knows how ill I might have become. So despite feeling very low, before Christmas I said, *Right, I need to change universities. I can't stay here – I need to get out.* I really put a lot of effort into finding the right university and the right course, so I chose Spanish at Leeds and they allowed me to transfer.

That is where it all started to get better. I went home that summer after that disastrous year in Glasgow and did some work in a local hospital. Thankfully I started to come back to being myself. I was still not eating much but over time there were signs of improvement in my health. I started going to the gym and changed my diet; gradually I began to feel better about my body image. Small steps, but it did start to improve. I was making a real effort to be a healthy, happy person.

When I started at Leeds it got even better. I ended up living with my best friend, Nicky, and a friend from school, called Louise, who owned a penthouse in the town. Nicky introduced me to gaming and all the sci-fi and fantasy geek stuff like *Lord of the Rings* – yes, I am a secret geek! – and we would sit in that flat for hours gaming, watching movies, having a great time. I met another great friend, Cat, who is a real life Bridget Jones, only prettier and thinner. We became this little gang just having a great time.

As I was feeling so much happier and healthier, I joined every university society that I fancied, the musical theatre society, the opera society, LGBT Society (Lesbian, Gay, Bisexual, Transgender), all sorts. The LGBT Society introduced me to a lot of other gay people that I had never come across before. I am not particularly camp and I don't really go out on the gay scene, so at times it felt quite hard for me to meet people. However, in Leeds I had a great circle of friends, some gay, some straight – it was brilliant. I even felt comfortable enough in myself to start a relationship.

I lived right next to Leeds market and I started shopping for food there and I got really into cooking. I was still very thin, but that was mainly because I walked everywhere, and I still hadn't increased my calorie intake to what it should have been. With each day of enjoying myself, my eating habits improved, then my health would benefit, so I'd feel happier and it started to become a really positive cycle. I regard that time as some of the best years of my life. Perhaps not surprisingly, my studies improved too.

As part of my Spanish course, I had to take a year abroad, so the following summer I moved to Madrid. Once again, my routines were changed overnight and at first I did struggle – I didn't know anyone, the city was new to me, I had no routines… it was a little precarious for a while. I was teaching English at a school and on the first day I walked in to the staff room and they were – obviously – chatting away in Spanish. Previously I'd thought I was pretty good at that language but I thought to myself, *What on earth are they talking about?*

Gradually, though, I started to settle in and I came to love Madrid. I think most cities need a year for them to really get under your skin. I didn't sing very much during that year, mainly because I was working three jobs – I taught kids in a school in a village in the mountains, I worked as an au pair twice a week and I also taught in a private language school. I eventually became completely fluent in Spanish and very much used to big cities. I came to really enjoy the Spanish culture, the food, the way of life and I met some fabulous people. I had a two-year long relationship during that time that broke up when I was there because of the distance. I made it through the year in Madrid and ultimately really enjoyed the whole experience. I was proud of myself for sticking with it and I'm glad I did, because it was very rewarding.

What I did miss terribly during my time in Spain was my musical theatre friends – singing, performing, and pursuing the dream. At times my anxiety bubbled up again but I think that was because I knew I wasn't using my voice. I wasn't making progress towards my ultimate goal of being a professional singer. I started to worry that I was getting older and I didn't want the opportunity of a singing career to pass me by simply because I was too old for certain roles, rather than being based on my ability to sing. So when I got back from Madrid, with a year to go in my degree at Leeds, I was more determined than ever to push my singing.

I immediately found a house in Leeds that I wanted to live in with Nicky, plus we had another friend from school, called Sophie, who shared with us. It was just a little terraced house in the Headingley student area of the city. It was nice; we redecorated the whole house and made it a really homely little place. We'd spend days just drinking a few cans, playing on games. It was such an escapism thing, sitting in your own little terraced house with your group of friends and not thinking about the outside world. I felt very comfortable around my housemates and to be honest, for the first few months I think I just had too much fun! I really wanted to make sure I had fun at university as well as studying, because it is a very specific time in your life when you can do that. Technically it was my 'third' year so I quickly realised I had to knuckle down and study for my finals. My work started to make sense to me, I began to understand the course and I was getting high marks.

Away from my studies, I'd joined a big band, which had a reputation as quite a prestigious group on the university circuit. That was brilliant and I loved every minute – singing again so regularly was such a relief to me. We did loads of functions and gigs; we even went on a small tour to France in April 2012 just before my exams started. We had a week on a tour bus getting absolutely hammered on French wine and it was brilliant, just the best of times. We did a wine-tasting trip one night but everyone came out trashed because no one spat the wine out!

When the final exams came around I cracked on with revision and eventually came out with a 2:1, which I am very proud of. I moved back home with Mum and got a job at the hospital where she is the Chief Executive. I did a 9-to-5 job at that hospital and there is a beauty in that routine. There was a beauty in getting up in the morning, having breakfast with my sister and heading into work. The money was guaranteed, we'd go home and put a movie on, I knew where I would be each day and the routine was reassuring. I can see why that is an appealing career. Ultimately, however, I wanted to be a singer and performing as a career is not normally well known for providing regular work!

It is at this point that I must mention a man called Graeme Danby who is an integral part of my story. He was originally a principal bass for the English National Opera and was educated at the Royal Academy, so he was a very well-known and highly respected singer. He heard me sing in a competition when I was 19, called 'Talent On The Tyne', which I had won. He decided to offer an extra prize, which was mentorship under him, which was just brilliant news. So that's what he did, he mentored me all the way through university. He was a brilliant teacher, I learnt so much from him it was incredible. Not only that, he has amazing contacts; he still is a really big name in Newcastle and indeed in the operatic world.

When I came home after my degree I was thinking of doing a diploma in singing, then Graeme told me about an opportunity at a place in Hammersmith, London, called The Associated Studios. It is an organisation that takes performers from opera or pop or whatever their genre is, and teaches them how to work in musical theatre. I really liked the sound of that because I felt I needed to be around the genre more – the musical theatre world is a lonely world if you are not working because you don't know people.

So suddenly I was moving down to London for this musical theatre conversion course. I was anxious, terrified in fact, I'm not going to pretend otherwise, but I think my time in Madrid had prepared me well and I was also just so eager to keep on plugging away at my singing until something happened.

I moved into a place in Willesden Green and, unlike Glasgow or the early days of Madrid, I quickly slotted into London life. I moved down to London in January 2013 and generally it was a great transition. Like I said, I was used to big cities by then and, let's face it, I was following my dream. I made some amazing friends, including an Australian called Liz who is now one of my best friends. I had a nice relationship with someone that eventually ended but that was good for me too. Financially it was a little precarious. I spent four months living off my savings that I'd built up over the years but then I had to get a job. My family has always worked in hospitals – Mum runs a hospital, my sister is training to be a doctor, my dad has worked with the patient network system – everyone is very involved in the NHS. So I got a job in the NHS. I also trained as a vocal coach so that I could earn extra money that way. That particular job also made sure I used my voice and kept it in good condition.

Then I moved to Shepherd's Bush to my first really nice place, a lovely maisonette that I shared with three other people. I was working hard at The Associated Studios and really enjoying life. All the time though I was conscious of finding new musical theatre work: *How do I get roles, who do I need to impress, where are they, when can I see them?* I am very driven and I never let up. Me being me, I researched every single agent and tried to find out who was the best one for my aspirations. In the musical theatre world, agents are your life; you need an agent to even get into an audition room. During my research, I came across this man called Shane Collins. He is a massive musical theatre agent, known by everyone, a big-time agent who only takes on people that he really finds interesting.

I thought to myself, *Well, maybe he will find me interesting,*

I'm tall and gangly, I've got an operatic voice… let's try. Shane is a lovely, lovely man, completely larger than life, and he agreed to see me. He called me in to his office and asked me to sing some opera but before I had chance to start he said, 'Darling, if I saw you in a club I would think you were fit, but if I saw you in an interview like this I would think you were an idiot.' I should explain that at the time I had my hair swept back and I had grey patches down the side, so he continued, 'I want you to cut your hair and look more like a younger man, not a young fop. Now sing me some opera.'

I stood there and sang 'Se vuol ballare' from *The Marriage of Figaro*, but I was so nervous that for some reason I started conducting myself like an orchestra. I don't know why I did that; I'd never done that before in my life!

Shane said, 'Darling, why on earth are you doing that, who conducts themselves? Honestly, get a grip, this is an audition, take your opportunity.'

So I did. I sang to him and he must've liked what he heard because he offered to take me on to his books. He is now one of my best friends and I adore him.

I started to feel the benefit straight away too, because he got me into auditions for *Les Misérables, Miss Saigon*, pretty much all the main shows. I didn't get them but even having a shot felt like several steps up the ladder. There seems to be a stigma against people who haven't done three-year courses or who aren't classed as what musical theatre people call 'triple threat' – performers who can dance, act and sing. Well, I can't really dance, actually, let's be honest, I am crap! I am not a typical musical theatre singer. I am tall and gangly, which limits the amount of roles I will be able to play. I have a tattoo – I wanted a tattoo even knowing that some people in musical theatre frown upon that and either won't employ you or they ask you to cover-up. (By the way, my tattoo says, 'You see but your shadow when you turn your back to the sun', a quote from Kahlil Gibran, a writer I love. I got that to commemorate Collabro's album being Number 1). So in many ways I don't tick a lot of the musical theatre boxes. Still, I've found a way around that, I guess.

Back then the rejections mostly just bounced off me. Not because I wasn't disappointed and at times disheartened, but because I was so determined to get there eventually. Just keep going. I started going to the gym, I was getting into really good shape, I was eating well, and I really started to feel like I was giving this my best shot. I was also working in a local hospital, doing some vocal coaching and teaching Spanish, so I had money coming in, which allowed me to keep plugging away. Even though I hadn't had any luck yet, I definitely sensed a momentum building.

After about a year of working with Shane on these auditions, I was told about a holiday company who needed a team of performers to entertain their holidaymakers abroad. The contract was for six months travelling around various hotels, entertaining the guests, doing one show a night for six nights on, one night off. They wanted two boys and two girls – tenor, bass, alto, soprano. You all had to be able to dance and sing. It was relatively well paid and I was very excited when I got the news that they wanted me for the job.

I say it was well paid but actually I was earning more money from my three jobs at home. I'd effectively created this little business of my own and I was earning well, teaching, vocal coaching and working at the hospital. I went from making about £2,000 a month to earning around £1,000. I didn't care though, because I knew the holiday company contract was a great opportunity to learn, to perform, to live overseas – it just felt like the right thing to do. After all, you never know who you might meet on jobs like that...

It turned out I was replacing someone who'd had a car crash, so me and a girl called Louise flew out to Cyprus and started work. We only had two weeks to learn all these shows and routines – it was barking mad! You perhaps won't be surprised to hear that the start of my latest adventure didn't exactly go to plan! I immediately fell very ill with some weird stomach bug I'd apparently caught off a parasite inside a partially frozen ice cube. I went to hospital and was on a drip for four days. Mum nearly flew out and at one point they thought I was at risk of renal failure – it was very serious. Thankfully they sorted that all out and I quickly recovered – I came out of hospital four days later and had to go straight back into rehearsal!

It was a great lifestyle out in Cyprus. I kept my flat in London because in Cyprus I didn't have to pay for accommodation. I had a lovely villa with a pool and I rescued some kittens too. I know, the things you do! They have all got lovely homes in England now.

Those hotel gigs were brilliant training because the crowds are not necessarily that easy. You have to really work hard to impress them. I was performing so frequently that my voice was really developing. I was using the gym on site in my time off, I was eating well, getting plenty of sunshine, going to the beach, having the odd cocktail – I really enjoyed myself.

When my time in Cyprus came to an end, I was sad to leave but also excited about getting back to London to hit the audition circuit again. My voice had evolved hugely and was really strong from performing six times a week. I was sitting at home at Christmas and I just thought to myself, *2014 is the year, it has to be.* Part of that was optimism, but another part of it was because I was getting a bit disenchanted, to be honest. After I'd returned from Cyprus I had another round of West End auditions but once again I didn't get any parts. I just wasn't getting the roles. I don't mind admitting at times I started to think, *Is this ever going to happen?* I didn't really have enough money to start my own business; I had some savings but they wouldn't last forever, I could go into vocal coaching full-time but if I did that my chances of performing professionally would be limited. Something needed to happen soon.

Don't get me wrong, I was proud of all my little jobs, my mini business. I would like to think I'd been a good student, I was a good teacher, a good vocal coach and I worked hard in the NHS, but the only time when I think I truly became myself was when I got on stage, stood in front of an audience, and felt the lights on me. I know that sounds rather dramatic, but it's just how I feel. So I was still completely obsessed with the idea of singing for a living. I had to find a way.

After Cyprus, I'd stayed in touch on Facebook with quite a few of the amazingly talented people who worked for the same holiday company. One of them was a lad actually based in Spain but who I'd met on social media and then become good friends with. He was a guy from Carlisle, called Matt Pagan.

CHAPTER 2

MATT

I loved being at home when I was a kid. We would always play games in our house – me, my mum and dad and my brother, altogether. Monopoly was my favourite. We also had a dog called Jip, this lovely Border collie, so if we weren't indoors playing games we'd go out for walks with the dog. We lived in Carlisle and there is a place nearby called Caldbeck – these beautiful hills in the countryside where we would always go to walk the dog or play in the snow or go sledging. Fantastic, happy memories.

I loved living in Carlisle. It's actually a very cultural city: there's a big castle, an amazing cathedral, museums and lots of cool places to eat and drink with pubs and restaurants dotted around. To me, as a kid, it felt really exciting and busy, although I suppose now that I live in London I can see it was fairly quiet by comparison. It's the only city in Cumbria and in relation to some parts of England it's fairly isolated, I suppose. That said, it has been voted one of the happiest places to live in Europe, and I'm not surprised. I have to say I never felt isolated as a kid. I loved growing up there.

My memories of my childhood are fantastic. My dad is a maintenance engineer at Pirelli and has worked there for over 30 years. He started there when he was 16 and still absolutely loves it, so he's in the right job and still has a passion for his work. My mum was a dinner lady at my primary school, which was really cool although I don't remember getting any extra servings or puddings! I *wish*. She had a spell working at Morrissons but she didn't really enjoy that so she went back to being a dinner lady, which, like my dad, she loves too. So they both have jobs that they really like.

I have an older brother, Michael, and we had a very close bond when we were kids. With us two in the house it was always very noisy. My brother and I would always be running around playing games like hide and seek or football, and messing about in the garden. We caused some mayhem when we were younger! We had quite a big garden and one year Dad bought us a set of football goals, which was brilliant. The only problem was the hedge between us and next door wasn't very high and with my brother being so rubbish at football – only joking, Michael! – the ball was constantly going over into their garden. We would always have to go round and sheepishly knock on the door to ask for the ball back. Occasionally they would say 'No!' so then you knew you'd done it too many times in one day. It was harmless fun though, just kids playing in their garden. It was great having Michael around, just having that person to mess about with.

My dad did shift work, but Mum would always be home in time to get my brother and me from school. We were all really close as a family – still are. I am proud and lucky to say that I had a very good upbringing. My parents have always been so supportive of everything I have done. My grandparents have always been involved too, as you will see. Later, when Collabro kicked off, my dad was very much up for me moving to London and following my dream, going for it. Mum didn't want me to move away, obviously (she cried when I eventually did), but looking back to when I was a kid, not once did she miss a chance to encourage me to follow my singing aspirations, even knowing that it would most likely take me away from her. I am very grateful and lucky to be able to say that.

I think maybe one reason I never felt isolated living in Carlisle when I was a kid is that we went on loads of brilliant holidays abroad. We went to Marmaris in Turkey about four times which was probably my favourite place. We went to Majorca, Crete, Greece, Malta and Bulgaria… I always looked forward to the school holidays because I knew we'd be going somewhere brilliant abroad.

Back at home, Dad played the cornet and I have one particularly fond memory of sitting around with my dad and my brother on the end of the bed, listening to him play to us. It was just a really nice, enjoyable feeling. Looking back, I think that is maybe when I first thought I wanted to be a musician.

I started playing the cornet myself soon after and my first experience of music as a performer came in the Salvation Army. Every Sunday my brother and I would go and play in the band there. Then I started to learn the trumpet, tenor horn and, in my later years, the guitar, drums and eventually piano would follow too. So I have always been very musical, ever since primary school age.

I am not going to lie, at that early age I wasn't really into the singing. They did a lot of singing at the Salvation Army and I went along to the singing events, but initially I wasn't really into it that much. Part of the problem back then was that I didn't like the limelight at all. The idea of a solo was horrendous, so I just used to enjoy sitting in the band playing my instrument. It was just shyness, nothing more complicated than that. The funny thing is, at home I tended to be the one at family gatherings who would always try to stand up and make people laugh. In that environment I would happily joke about and be the centre of attention, but not in public. During my younger years standing out of the crowd on stage was not something I was comfortable with at all.

I went to Belah Primary, and like most schools for that age group, we would do the nativity and all the traditional plays at Christmas. One year we did *Scrooge* and I played Bob Cratchit – just a speaking part. I didn't really get very nervous for that but then I think at primary school you are not exactly getting into character; at that young age you tend to be just reading words that you have memorised from a script. I was getting better at the cornet and trumpet, and I even had a solo one Christmas, which funnily enough didn't really bother me. I played a few wrong notes but hey, I was only about nine! I remember hitting all the right notes – it's just that some of them were in the wrong order, as they say.

I left Belah in 2004 and went to St. Aidan's county high school (now known as Richard Rose Central Academy), which I absolutely loved. It was amazing. It had a good sports complex with a big *Astro turf* pitch and tennis courts. I started singing in a few shows but still nothing as a soloist. I had a good mix of friends – both sporty mates and those that were into performing. I loved being at that school – it was brilliant. I've got such fond memories of my time there. We also got a new dog around this time, a working Cocker Spaniel called Joe. He has always been such a companion, a lovely dog and a real part of our family.

If I am being totally honest with you, when I was at secondary school I was quite cheeky. I wouldn't say I was a troublemaker as such, but I wasn't exactly the best child in class. When you get to secondary school, you are more self-conscious and you are more aware of what your mates think and what is perceived as 'cool'. Like I say I had a good bunch of mates but I worried it wasn't exactly considered cool to be singing and performing. So there was a spell when I was conscious of that and I felt like, *Do I want to be doing all this performing?* It wasn't like performing was all I did; I was really quite sporty as well. I was playing in the local football team with all my mates and later on I even did a bit of training for mixed martial arts. I played golf locally and my whole family was heavily into sport. My dad was – and still is – the manager of Stanwix FC, my local football team which I played in for 15 years.

I just wasn't always sure of myself and that meant sometimes I would try to impress people. It wasn't even that the other kids thought performing wasn't cool; it was *what I thought* they were thinking. Looking back, everybody in school knew I sang but nobody said anything negative to me. I never got bullied for singing. It was more about how I thought it would be perceived. I never really knew where I fitted in. There were the sporty kids and the musical kids, but I never knew where I belonged, so I guess I was always trying to impress the so-called 'cool' kids, sort of copy what they were doing.

You do get people at school who give other kids some stick, and I am not going to lie, occasionally I was one of them. I had a phase of not exactly being the nicest kid in school. I did give people grief in school sometimes – name-calling, that sort of stuff. That's just horrible.

We would just mess about, but sometimes you realise you'd go a bit too far. I would always go home and think, *Did I say that to them, really? I feel terrible.* I would never mean what I said, it was meant in jest but you realise that kids don't always take things like that and it upsets them. It was just my ill-judged way of trying to fit in, I guess. But listen, no excuses. Since I left school, I've in-boxed a couple of people on Facebook saying, 'I am really sorry, it wasn't very nice to do that and I just hope you know I didn't mean anything by it, I was just being an idiot.' They were really good about it; they said they understood I was young and it was fine. That was really nice to hear.

It was worrying about fitting in that made me still feel so shy about my performing during secondary school. The idea of a solo was still a nightmare to me! I remember there was one performance where we did 'Merry Christmas Everyone' with a big solo in the middle that I was supposed to play on the trumpet. We performed in front of each year separately and I was fine playing the solo in front of all the other years. However, when it came to my own year, when I was supposed to be playing in front of all my mates who were all sat in the first row, I just couldn't do it. I just felt embarrassed, shy, and self-conscious. I went up to my teacher and said, 'I just can't do this, I really can't.' So in the middle of the concert, I actually walked out. My dance teacher came and found me and said, 'Listen, Matthew, if you really don't want to stand up and do the solo that's fine, so how about you just sit in the orchestra and do the solo that way?' Funnily enough I was absolutely fine with that idea, so I did my trumpet solo sitting down. I could see a few people looking a bit bemused, because they could hear this solo but there was no one standing up! But it helped me with my shyness and it went okay.

Away from school, music was always a big part of family life. Aside from my dad playing the cornet, my grandad was a very good singer. He didn't do it professionally, but if he went into a pub someone would say, 'Alex is going to sing!' and he would stand up and do a song. He was a cracking singer. My dad is a brilliant singer too but he has never had the confidence to go out there and perform – he has always said that I am living the dream for him, because he always wanted to do it but never had the confidence.

Both my grandad and my dad were big into their swing music and their passion rubbed off on me. They were also both into their golf and twice a year our golf society still all go to a caravan park in Southerness, Scotland to play a few rounds. If the Ryder Cup is on we place a few bets and also compete against each other for trophies. I have really special memories of those trips. We go there and play a few rounds of golf, we all have lots to drink and then we sit in this little living area of the caravan and chat all night. Inevitably someone will start off the entertainment – it would normally be my grandad – he would say, 'Right, come on, let's have a song', and he would start singing unaccompanied. There will sometimes be as many as 12 lads sitting all around. I will sometimes chip in too. It's become a really lovely tradition, so much so that people prepare things for each visit – some will tell jokes, some will tell a funny story, it's brilliant. In the evening of the Saturday we will always go down to a nearby lighthouse and stand looking out to sea then our close family friend Mark Daley will say a prayer for absent friends or people who have passed. We always sing 'Oh Genevieve' and my dad will do the solo part in the middle. It is really emotional, such a lovely thing to do. So there is singing in the family, albeit not as a career.

My interest in singing really started to ramp up as I worked my way through my secondary education. I was appearing in various school productions and plays during those teenage years. When one of my school mates dropped out of his part in *The Little Drummer Boy* due to illness, I had to step in and I enjoyed that; it went alright and I wasn't as shy as I'd been before.

My first musical theatre show was a production of *Grease* when I was 15 and I played Roger, one of the T-Birds. That performance actually ended up having a pretty major impact on my career, or at least on my progress towards a career in singing and performing. That night in the audience was a fantastic couple called David and Sallie McNeill, who run this amazing theatre company called StagedRight. Their son, Jack, was in a youth theatre and I would often go and see shows so we bumped into each other now and then. Around the time I got that part in my first musical, *Grease*, I was on social media chatting with Jack. I'd recently seen him performing a song from *Billy Elliott* and I messaged him to say he was amazing and well done. I said I'd love to do something like that, and then told him about *Grease* and said, 'It'd be great if you could come along and have a look at the show!' He did and he also mentioned it to his parents who came along with him. As I said, this was my first musical so I was obviously pretty nervous but they seemed to like what they saw because afterwards they came and said hello and offered me a place in their youth theatre. I was over the moon about that, because StagedRight has such a great reputation as an award winning theatre company, it is so popular.

StagedRight instantly became a big part of my life. Every Friday night I would go there and throughout the year we'd all work on a big production. They taught us all about singing, dancing, acting, stage craft, and dialogue – we learnt so much. Over the year we'd perfect the routines and the show, and along the way we would also perform various concerts. Then in the summer holidays it was time for the big performance. As soon as I joined their youth theatre, I was straight into rehearsing for *Peter Pan*, which was my first show with them. I played an 'Unnamed Pirate'!

I have so much to thank StagedRight and David and Sallie for.

After *Peter Pan* I also appeared in *West Side Story*, *Me & My Girl* (I was Sir John, alongside their son Jack), *Beauty & The Beast* (I played the Baker, how ironic), as well as numerous concerts and cabarets. For each new production I stepped up – so from initially being the 'Unnamed Pirate', I gradually worked my way up until aged 17 I was Riff in *West Side Story*, which is one of the main parts. I remember we also did concerts at The Theatre by the Lake in Keswick, which were amazing. Another highlight was performing with the theatre at a concert to celebrate the arrival of the Olympic Flame in 2012, in front of a crowd of no less than 35,000 people. Walking on stage to that many people in front of you was just the most incredible feeling. We did 'Ain't No Mountain High Enough' and a James Bond medley. What a feeling! StagedRight was a *major* part of my life. It is where I learnt so much and it also fuelled my passion for musicals. I will always be hugely grateful to David and Sallie for everything they did for me in my time there.

I also appeared in various small productions at school, such as *Oliver!* playing the Artful Dodger, that was a fun show. At this point I tended to always get the 'cheeky chappie' type of roles, rather than the more serious lead parts. Then after that it was just odd concerts in school where I would sing solos. The first specific musical theatre performance that I remember doing was at GCSE level when I sang 'Bring Him Home' from *Les Misérables* at a concert in school. That would not be the last time that song had an impact on my life...

I'm not going to pretend that performing was all I ever wanted to do as a kid. In fact, for much of my childhood, I had a real passion for cooking and, actually, working in a professional kitchen was initially my main ambition in terms of a career. The big dream at the time was to be a chef – that is what I wanted to do. My grandad was a great chef. He never did anything professionally but he had a real passion for it so I think that's probably where I got my interest.

It was during secondary school that my interest in cooking really intensified. I always loved food technology classes, which I took to GCSE and did very well with. I loved learning all about the various foods, the ingredients, the intricate ideas and all the skills that chefs needed. I used to really look forward to those classes. Before I even took the exam though, I had been out and about working in actual kitchens, which I just adored.

I was still in school aged 14 when I did two weeks' work experience at the Cumbria Park Hotel in Carlisle. I absolutely loved working there, initially just learning how to do starters and desserts. I guess I must have made a decent impression, because they kept me on working on a Saturday. After a few weeks of that, they asked me if I wanted to work Sundays as well, which I snapped up. I remember thinking, *I really like doing this!* I just found it fascinating and I loved the atmosphere in the kitchen – the team, the banter – I loved everything about it. To be honest, we had a great team and I am still in touch with the head chef now. They were a very caring bunch.

For the next year I worked increasingly longer hours, so I was pretty much doing it full-time in the end, working nearly every day. I would finish school and go there for about 6pm, working through till 10pm. Eventually I was made redundant from the Cumbria Park Hotel. The head chef left too and then one day he rang me up and he asked me to join him working at two other pubs, The Bay and The Coach And Horses in Carlisle. That was really nice, I was really proud that he'd asked me to join him again. When he later left there and went to work at another place, he asked me to join him again.

MATT

There is this perception of professional kitchens that everyone works really long hours and that they are not very nice places to be, with chefs screaming and shouting at people. Well, there are very long hours, for sure, but my experience was just fantastic, it was such a great team and I loved every minute. Obviously you do make mistakes and you will get shouted at sometimes. If you do something wrong when they are really busy you will get told off because there is a lot of pressure and you are always in a rush to serve the customers. I did get shouted at a couple of times. For example, I knew sea bass was really expensive to buy but I didn't know that you're not supposed to batter and fry it! One night I managed to do that and they did, of course, shout at me. It was funny though, because although they obviously couldn't serve it to the customers, after the service had ended they tasted it and said it was really good! In fact, if it hadn't been so expensive, I think they might've even put it on the menu!

My time working in kitchens was great fun and I still miss that now. However, during that period, my passion for performing really started to take over my life. As much as I enjoyed working in the kitchens, I did start to think, *Is this what I want to do as a career though?* By then I'd been appearing in all these local productions and loving it more and more each time. I couldn't get enough of performing and so that just became my absolute top priority. I'd started to get a lot of praise for my performances and began to think, *Maybe I can make a career out of this instead?*

I'm actually very proud to say I worked on the pub and club circuit around Cumbria for three years, performing swing music. Talk about an apprenticeship! It was just my dad and me on the road; he would take me around, help me set up, arrange everything, and do the sound – he was brilliant. There aren't many pubs and clubs in the area that I haven't done. My dad has always been by my side; we have always been a team. I loved that part of it. I dedicated so much time to working the pubs and clubs. Plus I was making a bit of money too, which was always welcome! Eventually, with my performances and club work ramping up all the time, I gave up the idea of being a chef to pursue the dream of being a singer.

At 16, I wasn't actually old enough to be getting into pubs and clubs. It was a baptism of fire at times; I did feel uncomfortable on occasion. Not in terms of safety, but in terms of wondering whether anyone would even listen. In the pubs especially, people are there to have a drink, so sometimes you'd do your entire set and people wouldn't even turn around to look at you. That is quite tough on your confidence at times. I was also very young to be playing the circuit, especially with swing music – that was really unheard of, to be honest. I was always nervous, I'd turn to Dad and say, 'I dunno, Dad, this crowd looks pretty hard, I don't think I wanna do this one,' but he would always say, 'Will you calm down, Matt? Just get on with it; they will love it once you start singing, just crack on! You know you can do it, just get on with it.' Of course, I always did go on stage and every single time it went down really well but no matter how many times I'd done one of these gigs, I still had that little moment before I went on when I would panic and be like, 'I don't want to do it!' It was almost a part of my ritual.

I had a great time doing those clubs, despite the tough audiences, but I also began to feel ever more drawn to a life in musical theatre, with the ultimate goal of performing in the West End. In fact, by this point, I was pretty much obsessed with a career in musical theatre. Thoughts of being a chef had passed by and I just wanted to become a professional performer. The swing gigs brought in some money, and the StagedRight shows and lessons were teaching me so much stuff all the time, so it was all heading in the right direction. At the same time, there was no obvious door opening, not yet, so I just kept plugging away. I have to admit, my studies did suffer really, because by that point I was doing A Levels but I was dedicating so much time to performing. Generally the studies came second, if I'm being totally honest. For example, when we were doing *West Side Story* with StagedRight, I had an exam in the morning and a tech run for the production in the afternoon and I literally just raced through this exam paper as fast as I could just so I could get to StagedRight as soon as possible!

It was around this time that I first bumped into an agent called Phil McKay who runs a company, called Lakeside Castings Agency, in Carlisle. He'd previously been on TV with shows such as *Pick A Number* on Grampian in Scotland, and since then he'd established this really great agency near where we lived. I'd previously come runner-up in a local competition called 'We've Got Talent' at the Sands Centre in Carlisle in 2009 (coincidentally, that was the same venue where, in 2015, Collabro would be starting their first ever headline tour). Phil had seen me perform there and he approached me and said he wanted to help get my name out there. He invited me to his office and when I got there he asked me to sing, right there and then, no backing track, in front of him. I was petrified to be honest. I knew of Phil locally, he was a big name agent and everyone really respected him, so that was quite an intimidating moment! I did my best and he seemed to be impressed because he took me on to his books. Lakeside Castings also ran some acting workshops, which were great, and Phil was so very well connected and experienced.

He promised to get me some gigs and that's exactly what he

did. My first job was at Stanwix Park Holiday Centre in Silloth. There had been quite a big build-up to the first gig there because I was starting to get my name known around Carlisle a little bit, so I'd been on the radio promoting my first solo show, and it was in the local paper (I have still got the clippings at home!) 'Matthew's about to hit the big time!' I had rehearsed and rehearsed so I was well prepared, but it was still a big deal – I was very nervous. They were really welcoming at the holiday park and after arriving they even showed me through to my own dressing room. I can distinctly remember standing in front of the mirror, I had a white shirt on, a loose bow tie dangling down my chest and a smart suit, and I just remember looking at the mirror and saying to myself, *This is it, Matt, this is it*. It felt really important. It was, to be fair – that was a big moment in my life. My first big concert out on my own.

I sang my heart out and got a great reception. I was so pleased – it was amazing. I opened with 'Cry Me A River', the Michael Bublé version – so no pressure! – and I also did 'Mack The Knife', 'Fly Me To The Moon' and 'Ain't That A Kick In The Head'. I always ended my shows with 'My Way', and there is a very special reason why I do that, which I will come back to later.

Anyway, back in 2009, I'd started doing all these solo gigs and things were going really well. Then Phil got in touch with a really well-known Cumbrian comedian called Lester Crabtree, who owns his own agency as well – Clubland Entertainments – and because of that I started to get solo gigs outside of Carlisle. So I started singing much further afield, places like Barrow, all over the county really. I was working so hard because Cumbria is a big place!

However, although the performing was going well, I still wasn't earning enough money to sing full-time, so once I was out of school I had to think about a job. My uncle works at a kitchen shop called

Andersons in Denton Holme in Carlisle and he knew someone nearby in retail that had been to China and bought a load of these electric bikes. So a big sign went up outside a shop saying 'Eco-pedal power is here!' They needed someone to sell these electric bikes and I needed a job so I went for that and before I knew it, I was sitting in this shop all by myself from 9 to 5 (usually with a laptop next to me with a movie playing during quiet periods), trying to sell these bikes. To be fair, I didn't know the first thing about selling bikes, I'd ridden bikes before, of course, but as far as knowing any technical details I didn't really have a clue. My sales patter tended to consist of me giving people a leaflet and saying, 'Do you want to buy a bike?'

Then the kitchen place said they needed someone to start doing internet sales, so they approached me and said, 'We need someone who is good on a computer and can chat to people, do you want the job?' and I thought, *Why not? I will give it a go!* So I started selling kitchens in the day and doing all my gigs at night. It was hard work and long hours but I loved it. I was still selling the electric bikes on eBay too, so I thought I was quite the salesman! There was a guy upstairs called Derek who would help me out if I needed it but essentially I was on my own all day selling kitchens. Like the bikes, I didn't really know the first thing about kitchens, so people would come into the shop and ask me all these questions and I have to be honest, I kinda made it up as I went along. 'Yes, certainly madam, these kitchen units are very strong, in fact they are dragon-proof!'

I did that for about a year and even though it wasn't my dream job, I did actually enjoy it. Having to sell all day actually boosted my confidence, because I found myself becoming increasingly able to chat with anyone. It really gave me that ability to have a bit of banter and make conversation with anyone who walked through the door.

I was still performing as often as I possibly could. Another job I got during this time was playing the part of Wishy Washy in *Aladdin* for The Panto Company, near Bedlington in Newcastle. My friend Mike was playing the part of Aladdin and at the last minute the guy cast to play Wishy Washy was taken ill, so Mike rang me up and asked if I could fill in. I asked 'When do we leave?' to which he replied, 'Er, tomorrow, Matt!' so I packed a bag and headed over to meet them the next day. He emailed me the script and I had just four days from that phone call to the first performance so it was a bit of a mad rush to learn all the lines. We performed around various children's hospitals and hospices. I loved it – we had such a brilliant time. There was literally just the four of us, we carried around the whole set in a van and put it up at each venue, hauling these heavy metal poles with cloth back-drops, then we'd carry the speakers in and all the equipment – there was some heavy lifting involved! We used to stay at little country B&Bs or the odd hotel and a couple of people would take it in turns driving while the others caught up on some sleep. It was hectic but fantastic. I loved every minute.

It was great fun once we were on stage too. We'd perform the usual pantomime songs but also the odd pop song like 'Time of my Life' from *Dirty Dancing* and 'Barbara Streisand' by Duck Sauce, just really fun songs to perform in front of all these kids. The show was full of daft, silly jokes and the kids just giggled the whole way through. The audiences were such a big part of why I enjoyed that job – these were kids in hospitals and hospices, so they were really quite ill, some terminally, yet they laughed and cheered and loved every minute of it. Sometimes if there were kids who were too ill to make it down to the performance, we'd go up and meet them and try to brighten their day. That was tough, because seeing these kids who were so ill or knew they weren't going to get any better was really hard. I know it sounds like a cliché, but however tired I was or if something had been annoying me that day, meeting these kids was always such a great leveller, they were always so bright and positive and strong. You'd just think, *What am I fed up about? Matt, you think you have problems?* We toured all around the UK, it was such a good time, I was getting paid, doing what I loved, meeting all these amazing kids and performing with a really nice bunch of people. Happy times.

By now, I had done the pubs and clubs for ages and ages and I was getting kind of tired of that. I wanted to do more theatre, especially musical theatre. During the Christmas of 2012 I was sitting in the pub with my agent Phil and he said, 'Matt, I promise you that next year is going to be your year; this is going to be it. I am going to get you something big in 2013.' It was coming up to New Year and, sure enough, early in January Phil told me he'd got an audition for me for a big contract. The company in question was a holiday firm and they had seen my showreel that Phil had sent and he'd also called them up and said, 'You really need to hear this guy.' They seemed to agree because they'd phoned him back the very next day, asking to see me in London. Phil phoned me with the news and I was obviously really excited.

'Fantastic news, so when is the audition then, Phil?'

'It's tomorrow, Matt!'

It was so exciting. I'd only ever been to London once before, when I went with the school to see *Oliver!* so this was a big deal for me just travelling down to the capital. On that secondary school trip, we were going to see the West End performance so that we could improve our own version back in Cumbria. At the time, my drama teacher had said to me in the theatre, 'Which part do you want to play? Bill Sikes or The Artful Dodger?' and obviously I'd gone for the latter, one million per cent. Fast-forward to 2013, and this audition was in the very same theatre.

Like I say, this London audition was for a really big holiday firm who needed performers for their hotels around the world. It was a well-paid contract and very prestigious. So I travelled down and stayed with one of Phil's friends the night before. I turned up nice and early at the Dance Attic Rehearsal Studios in Fulham for the audition, where I sang 'Why God Why?' from *Miss Saigon* and 'How Sweet It Is (To Be Loved By You)', first recorded by Marvin Gaye. We also had to sing 'Love Changes Everything' from *Aspects Of Love* as a four-part harmony, which was great. After that I headed home and waited for the news from the audition.

I was sitting in the kitchen appliance showroom a few days later when the phone rang and it was Phil. He didn't mention the Spain audition and instead said he had got a TV show that wanted my parents and me to go on. It all seemed a little vague, and he said they needed to get a photo of the three of us together that evening. I said, 'No problem', and rang my parents and arranged to meet with them and Phil at a nearby hotel.

When we got there Phil was really bright and in a great mood. He took the photo of the three of us together and started talking about how he enjoyed working with me and then he started saying, 'You know, Matt, there are so many agents that don't actually tell their clients the truth, they promise all this stuff about getting work but it never comes off, then they say all sorts of things to get out of it... just telling lies really. I hate all that.'

'Yeah, sure, I know that, Phil,' I said, a little bemused.

'Well, Matt, I have to admit something now. I have been telling you a complete lie too.'

'Right...' I wasn't entirely sure where this was going because I trusted Phil 100 per cent.

'You know that TV job I told you about? That was completely made up.'

Then he turned to my mum and dad and said, 'How amazing would it be for you two to fly out to Spain to see Matt perform?'

My mum and dad's eyes lit up.

'Well, that is exactly what is going to happen... Matt... you got the job!'

I could've cried on the spot, it was so exciting. How fantastic that Phil chose to tell us that way, he took all that time to get us together so he could tell us in person when he could've just phoned up with the good news. That's the sort of man he is though. Fantastic, it was such a cool way to find out. I was absolutely overjoyed.

It was quite big news on the entertainment circuit in Carlisle. In fact, the local ITV News ran a piece about me getting the job, which they titled 'A Cumbrian teenager is swapping his day job as a kitchen salesman for a summer in showbiz performing on stage on the continent.' They sent a camera crew who filmed me singing and also working at the kitchen showroom. At the end of the clip, the interviewer asked me, 'Do you think when you've had your seven months come November, do you think you'll be back selling kitchens in Carlisle?' to which I replied, 'I hope not, I mean, I love working there but it is performing I want to do and hopefully something will come of this...'

Over 200 hopefuls had gone for the Spain contracts so I was really proud to have been picked; it felt like a big moment, as if my career had taken several steps up the ladder. The plan was to go over to this beautiful hotel in Spain where I'd be based, then perform several times a day for the guests; we would have to do game shows, cabaret, chat to the guests by the poolside, it was full-on but sounded so exciting. It was decent money too – at this point I felt that things really started to look up because I had this guaranteed wage for the next half-year. It was great work, out in sunny Spain, it just felt like it was the start of something really good.

Right before I went to Spain, my agent and I wanted to do a farewell show in Carlisle. So we produced a show at the Swallow Hill Hotel in Carlisle in their beautiful ballroom, billed as 'An Evening with Matthew Pagan and Friends'. It was brilliant fun. I had loads of my performer friends join the bill, I did a couple of duets, there was a dance company that performed, I did a monologue from *Blood Brothers*, then my own full set. There were loads of people there and we all had a great time. It was a fantastic send-off.

So off I flew to Spain. There was only me and three other people based at The Yaramar hotel in Fuengirola on the Costa Del Sol. We stayed at these apartments nearby, the accommodation was good, the hotel was amazing and I knew I was going to love it as soon as I arrived. The contract was with a company who tended to attract older customers and, mainly because of my amazing grandad, I have always found older people really fascinating, they just have so many brilliant stories and so much life experience. So for me it really couldn't have been any better.

In the day we would play beach games with the customers like horseshoe toss, giant Connect Four, quoits, water polo, afternoon quizzes, that sort of thing. We had a speaker fixed on top of a trolley – we called it 'The Anchor' – and we would make announcements throughout the day about what was happening next. For much of the day I would just walk around the pool chatting to people. Sometimes I'd have a few spare hours to go to the gym. There was a really good nightlife there too for the occasional evening off. It was just absolutely fantastic.

The shows were great fun to perform. We sang opera and musical theatre. We also did a 'Best of British' show, which featured anything from The Beatles to James Blunt. We had to sing in Spanish and Italian; we had to learn all of that as well. What a buzz.

I met the most amazing people over there. One day I'd overdone it in the gym and hurt my back, so one of my colleagues cheekily announced it on the PA system, 'Matt's hurt his little back in the gym so he can't play water polo today, aahhhh...' just having a bit of fun. Then this guy came over to me and said, 'I've heard you've hurt your back, what's the problem exactly?' I was a bit taken aback but I showed him anyway and then he said, 'There's a physio table in the gym, let's get in there and I will have a look.'

'Er, that's great,' I said, 'do you do physio work then?'

'Yes, I used to be part of the Welsh FA set-up, so I've worked on Gareth Bale, Ryan Giggs, all that lot.'

I was like, 'Okay then! Good enough for me!'

He put me on this table and then suddenly CRACK! My back was fixed, amazing.

I especially liked sitting with the older customers around the pool, chewing the fat, hearing their stories, and listening to their thoughts about life. After our performance in the evening, I would often go and get myself a Baileys from behind the bar and just pull up a chair and chat to these older people for hours. I have always been so close to my grandparents so it was really natural and enjoyable. The whole experience in Spain was just incredible. It really was amazing and I was having the time of my life.

Then my mum rang and told me that my grandad had cancer.

I was on my way to work when the phone rang and Mum told me not to worry, that he had gone into hospital, that he had cancer in his pancreas but that they were going to take it out and he could well be fine. Now, I am a worrier anyway so it wasn't very easy to be calm about this. As you now know, I worshipped my grandad and yet here I was, miles away in Spain. Mum insisted I didn't need to come home, that they were trying to sort it out. I convinced myself that he would be alright and tried to carry on working to the best of my ability.

A few days later Mum rang again and explained that the cancer had already spread to his liver, but again she said, 'Try not to worry, Matthew', and that it might be just fine. I asked her to keep me up-to-date by the minute. Less than a week went by and the phone rang again. This time it was my dad. He said, 'Matthew, you asked me to tell you if your grandad was getting seriously ill and whether you needed to come home… well, I think if you can, you should come home.'

My bosses were really good and even though it didn't actually qualify as compassionate leave, they gave me 48 hours off. I flew back to Manchester and my mum and dad picked me up at the airport, then on the way home we stopped at a service station. My dad said, 'Look, Matthew, I wanted to tell you in person, they've said your grandad has only got three months to live.' I was so gutted, absolutely devastated. This was a man who had played a huge part in my life, both in terms of my musical influences and also just as a man.

I went to visit my grandad in The Eden Valley Hospice where he was moved to and I am so grateful that I got that opportunity. He was amazing. Although he was really ill by then he was still joking about, charming everyone and flirting with the nurses. What an amazing man. I'm sure that's where I get my cheekiness. I stayed with him as long as I possibly could... and I got to say goodbye. That was a very emotional time. One of the last things he ever said to me was, 'Matthew, keep making me and your grandma proud, I love you.'

I had to fly back to Spain where I was performing the same day. That was hard, I'm not gonna lie, being all cheerful with the guests, many of whom were the same age as my grandad. All the time in the back of my mind I was thinking about Grandad and how he was doing. Another week went by and mum phoned to say he had deteriorated and that they thought it would be that day, so I said, 'Please let me know as soon as you hear any news, if my phone rings out, then I might be performing so just send me a text.'

Nothing happened throughout the day but I was worrying constantly, on edge all the time waiting for my phone to go. That week I was getting on really well with these two particular older guests (that I'm still in contact with now) and I was sitting next to them by the pool later in the day watching this comedian with them and just chatting. Then I felt my phone vibrate in my pocket. This one guest was telling me a story so I obviously didn't read the text because it would've been really rude, but as soon as it was appropriate I said, 'I'm really sorry, do you mind if I go and make a phone call please?'

I went into the games room for some privacy and read the text from my brother Michael. I rang him and when he told me Grandad had gone, my world fell apart. I was devastated. I was a long way from home, from him, from Grandma, from my parents. Luckily I didn't have to perform that night, but one of my colleagues saw I was obviously really upset and asked after me. I explained what had happened and she arranged with everyone to cover for me. They were so nice to me.

I ran home to my apartment and as soon as I walked through the door I just broke down crying. I packed a small bag and got to the airport, then flew back home. We had the funeral and then I had to fly back to Spain and perform the next night again. It was a tough time. That was a massive low point for me. One of my biggest musical influences was my grandad. He was such a great singer and as I mentioned before, he would always sing at his local and when we went away on those golfing breaks. Do you remember I said I always sing 'My Way' last at my solo gigs? And how that was my grandad's favourite song? Well, 'My Way' was indeed his song, he always sang it and so when I started performing I would always end with that too. While I was in Spain I got a tattoo on my chest that says, 'I faced it all and I stood tall and did it my way, Grandad'. Whenever I perform that song, I will always pat my chest over that tattoo, look up and think of Grandad. What a man.

Grandad must've been looking out for me because after Spain things just kept getting better. Towards the end of that superb contract overseas, I received a phone call from a man called Jonathan Higgins, who is the entertainment manager at the Sands Centre in Carlisle. He said he'd got a panto coming up at Christmas, *Snow White & The Seven Dwarfs*, and that he really wanted me to play Prince Lorenzo. Better still, he said he wanted to fly out to Spain to see me perform, which would be my audition (I have a lot to thank him for, he got me a lot of work and is a great friend).

So he did. He flew out and we met up, then he watched a show and a few days later he rang me up and said I had got the part. That was really exciting and the fact that there was no break in work just felt like there was a real career momentum building. So when

Spain finally came to a very reluctant end, I went straight home and started doing this panto.

I'd only been back a few weeks when rehearsals started. It was a great cast too, with Maureen Nolan as the Wicked Stepmother, Ben Hanson from *Tracy Beaker* as the Henchman, and a guy called Robbie Dee, who is a very well-known radio presenter in Cumbria, who had the comedy part. He was just hilarious and a really nice guy too. The whole cast was lovely and I had the best time. I was also pleased because for the first time I was playing the straight role rather than a comedy part. That was amazing, I loved doing panto. It was just an all-round great experience.

I really felt by now that there was a progression with my career. I was regularly in the papers, I had tons of club work, I'd done the Spain contract, then the panto, and I was getting an increasingly high profile. Looking back, once I had got over the shock of losing my grandad, his memory had inspired me and galvanised me so I was more determined than ever to make this work. I feel like he's really looking out for me.

While I had been working in Spain, I'd met various people who were also out in Europe working for the same company. We all tended to chat on Facebook and one of these guys was an amazing singer who'd been touring around Cyprus. We became friends online and when I eventually heard him sing, I was completely bowled over by what an incredible voice he had. His name was Jamie Lambert.

CHAPTER 3

TOM

My childhood was spent in a fairly rural part of Lincolnshire, soundtracked by tractors, farms and livestock. My parents split up when I was four so I spent my time divided between my mum's home in the week, in a little place called Donington-on-Bain, and my dad's in Saltfleetby. Mum's house was actually in a wood next to a field full of cows and sheep while Dad's village was over-run by tractors. At that very young age, it was good being out in the middle of nowhere because we always had dogs and cats and we could just let them wander off. It was nice for them to have that freedom. As I grew older, I sometimes felt a little bit more isolated but certainly during my primary school years at least, it was a lovely place to live.

I don't remember my parents' separation impacting on me as much as it might, say, on a teenager. I can't really remember much that far back, but I do recall that going to my dad's at the weekend just felt normal to me. I never really questioned it and no one ever brought it up at school. So I'm not even sure you could say I was upset by my parents' separation, I was just too young.

My dad has always been an agricultural engineer and one of the things I vividly remember from my childhood is him picking me up or dropping me off at Mum's, because when I got in his van it had this strong smell of oil from his tools and all his work gear. I used to enjoy sitting up in his van, bouncing along the country roads on the way back to Mum's, ready for school on Monday mornings. If it was very early, I'd still sometimes be in my pyjamas and dressing gown for the journey back to Mum's on Monday mornings. At certain times of the year it would be twilight and I'd be chatting away with my dad, just the two of us. He'd be playing his favourite bands on the car stereo; those are really fond memories. It's really funny how the mind works, because I find that oily smell oddly reassuring as an adult; it certainly brings back happy memories.

Dad worked for the same company for about 25 years, then he moved to a new firm, also local, that specialises in forklifts and equipment like that. He's not musical himself but he does enjoy listening to music. He was into all the bands such as Slade, T Rex and Mudd. In fact, the first gig I ever went to was Slade, with Dad. He would play those bands in the van whenever we were driving about. I got to really enjoy those bands, specifically the amazing voices of people like Marc Bolan and Noddy Holder. I realise those bands are from an older generation but whenever I am chatting to someone about music and they haven't heard of them, I'm like, 'How can you *not* have heard of Slade?' They're just fantastic bands and I'm sure that the connection with my dad and being around him listening to that music helped to reinforce that connection with those songs in my mind.

My mum had fairly eclectic tastes in music because on the one hand she has always loved classical music but she was also into the American rock band Extreme and groups like that. When she later met my stepdad, he was in the local choir, St James, in Louth, and also in an amateur dramatic society called The Louth Playgoers. I started going to the choir from an early age and continued to do so for about six years, during which time all that singing really shaped my voice. They did two services each Sunday but I only usually sang at one because otherwise it would've really cut into my time with Dad. I really enjoyed the people at choir and I loved the singing. I loved The Louth Playgoers too. Mum sang a little bit so she really enjoyed their performances and shows and we would all go together which was nice. I used to sit in the audience and be enthralled by some of the shows and musicals. At one particular show, my stepdad had a part and one of his lines was 'Certainly, certainly my pleasure,' and when it came to that sentence, I said it out loud with him from the audience, which caused quite a chuckle.

Fairly quickly, just watching the shows graduated into me being cast in small pantomimes and musicals. My first major performance was in the Arthur Miller play called *All My Sons*. I had a minor role, playing this little boy called Bert. I only had two scenes, one of which was with the central character called Mr Keller. He was played by a local man and I could never remember his actual name, so forever after that play and throughout my childhood I always used to refer to him as Mr Keller!

There wasn't really a lot of performing in my family before that point. My dad loved his music but only as a listener, he didn't sing himself. Mum sang a little bit but again, not professionally. However, when I started going to see these shows, I just loved listening to the singing and being in the choir, just performing in general. I preferred singing to acting, if I am being honest – singing was my passion. I just grabbed hold of it and, as is my nature, when I find something I really like, I get heavily into it. I don't remember if anybody ever said, 'Oh, that kid has got a really good voice, he needs to be doing something with that', I think people just encouraged me and I flourished.

The Louth Playgoers were pretty productive, putting on plays, musicals and pantomimes. So as I grew up I was around or actually involved in quite a few amateur dramatic shows. I did *Great Expectations*, I played the lead in *Oliver!* when I was 11, we also did *Camelot* and *South Pacific* as well as pantomimes such as *Dick Whittington*. It was great experience and they were a really nice bunch of people to be around. As each show came along I was just getting more and more into performing and although it was hard work in terms of hours – I would go to school all day then go straight to lengthy rehearsals in the evening – I didn't care, I loved it. As soon as I left one rehearsal, I'd be thinking, *When is the next one?*

As I grew up you will see that my musical tastes have been very varied, spanning literally dozens of genres. However, musical theatre seems to have been a constant. From early in my primary school years to the present day in Collabro, one genre that I have never tired of and have always wanted to be involved in is musical theatre.

However, it certainly wasn't any kind of career aspiration at that point. I was only about seven when I first started performing so any thoughts like that were some way off. However, as I went through school, the passion for singing grew and as you get older you do start to wonder what you might do for a job when you are an adult.

My primary school years are full of good memories. I wasn't

particularly a standout pupil; I was good at most things, but certainly not top of the class. I spent a lot of time drawing very elaborate borders around my work that I thought were great but didn't necessarily win me extra marks from the teachers! I wrote poems and sketched little bits of art on scraps of paper, I was always doing stuff like that and I got told off quite a bit for it. I was quite into my art at that age although it dropped off as I got older. I got on in school and I did my lessons – like I said I wasn't the best pupil there but I really kind of enjoyed it, especially music or drama because increasingly they were the things that I really wanted to do. I wasn't very academic so when I got to an age when you start thinking about jobs, I thought the only route that I really wanted to take was performing. I didn't really know anyone who was already in professional musical theatre or indeed anyone who openly wanted to pursue performing as a career. Everyone I knew was mostly the same age as me and still didn't really know what they were doing with their lives.

I was a very, *very* quiet child. Actually I'm still quiet, most people would class me as an introvert and I'd find that hard to argue with. My dad is very laid-back and I kind of get that side of my personality from him. Nothing much really fazes me. There are times where I can be very outgoing, but generally it is in my nature to be quiet and laid-back. Nonchalant, I think that's perhaps the best word.

During my later primary school years I discovered something that has since been a very major part of my life: gaming. I had always been quite heavily into video games, I had all the usual consoles like the Nintendo and Gameboy and I remember getting *Mario* for the first time, which was a great game. However, when I discovered a whole generation of role-playing games, for me pioneered by the

Japanese Role Playing Game (RPG) series, *Final Fantasy*, I was smitten. Maybe it was a part of my relatively isolated rural location, it was certainly appealing to my introverted nature, but I found these amazing role-playing games just incredible. They had these huge, epic storylines in these vast worlds that you could spend ages exploring, there was varied character development and intricate plot arcs, incredible graphics and back-drops, it was just amazing. These weren't banal shooters just blasting everything that walks in front of you; these were complex, multi-layered stories that just completely fascinated me. I was totally drawn in from the age of about eight. Gaming was my escapism then and it still is to this day.

I had a good friend who was also into gaming and we used to play for hours. It was really good to have that connection with somebody over something we both loved. I didn't have any siblings until I was about ten. My mum and my stepdad then had a son called Gabriel who was always full of beans and the amount of games that I lost because they were scratched or broken was crazy! Three years after that my dad and my stepmum had a daughter called Bethany and another nine years later they had a son called Ben. As I write this, Ben is six years old and is completely obsessed with tractors, so he's living in the right place! He watches them go past the house and gets very excited.

Being an introverted kid – into musicals, choir, singing and gaming – I guess secondary school was always going to present a bit of a challenge. I have to admit the transition from primary was a weird one. Being blunt, because I was quiet, I did get picked on quite a bit. I wasn't bullied extensively and it wasn't anything physical that I can remember, but I did get teased a lot.

One issue, which really didn't help, was the fact I suffer from quite severe Irritable Bowel Syndrome, known as IBS. That really kind of worried me as a child. It really panicked me, because I didn't want things to go wrong in class, so I was in and out of the toilet quite a bit. I got teased quite a lot for that, there was some pretty cruel name-calling.

I wasn't particularly sporty, which I know can help some kids fit in at school. I was also quite small and not very well built, so that didn't help either. Eventually, when I was 16, I started going to some kung-fu classes with a friend and I really enjoyed that. I went for a couple of years and did a few belts – that was great. The teacher would always talk about Chinese language and philosophy, which I found really interesting. Necessarily he would also always push us to spar, but I didn't really enjoy that part at all. Instead I enjoyed learning the techniques, the language, and the culture behind the skills. There was a series of movements called 'forms' and I'd do those for ages, but then the teacher would say, 'You've done enough of those now, Tom, you need to spar,' and I never really wanted to. However, going to those classes was great because it was the first thing that got me into some kind of physical shape. You might think this was also useful as a deterrent to the bullies at school, but to be honest I don't think I even told anyone that I was doing martial arts. I'm very much the kind of person that if somebody doesn't ask, I won't say anything. I'm very private.

Perhaps not surprisingly, gaming became an even bigger part of my life during secondary school. The games I am most drawn to are, like I said before, these epic, 60-hour sagas, which if you really get into them can take up a lot of your time. I have spent so much time playing these epic games! To be fair, I think a lot of people have preconceptions about gaming and gamers. For example, I know a lot of people who would think nothing of coming home after work, having dinner then sitting down and watching TV for three hours. That might be a soap, a drama, a film, whatever. Other people escape into a book all evening. I don't really see how that is any different in terms of escapism to me sitting down and playing something like *Dark Souls* for three hours in a night.

To be honest, the escapism element of gaming wasn't something that I consciously thought about. I just did it because I enjoyed it. I really enjoyed it. I have not got an addictive personality about anything – I don't drink, I don't watch much TV – but I have to be honest and admit that with games it is a different story. I will spend hours working through a story, then someone else will say they've already finished and I'll be like, 'Yes, but have you collected absolutely *everything*?' Gaming is the only place where I am really anal and have a really addictive, obsessive personality.

Someone asked me recently if I ever seriously thought about a career in gaming but to be honest, I didn't. It was always recreational for me. I guess I did wonder how these games were created and what it must be like to work in the games industry, but realistically, living in rural Lincolnshire, the chances of that becoming a viable career were minimal. Besides, the main idea for my future was always performing. I enjoyed – and still enjoy – games and they are a big part of my life in my spare time but as an actual career I wanted to be singing.

I say I wanted to sing as a career, but in my secondary school years it wasn't like I had some grand master plan of how I was going to achieve that. I don't tend to think too far ahead. I am always very much in the moment, 'Okay, what are we doing tomorrow?' rather than knowing in my head about every day of the next four weeks or whatever. It just makes it easier for me if I don't start worrying about events that far ahead. I think I always subconsciously knew what would be the next step, at least in terms of education – *Okay, I am in school, the next step is college, then the next is university…* and so on. I didn't consciously worry about how I was going to get into the music industry at that early stage; I was just really enjoying performing.

Later in secondary school I also started to join local bands. You might be surprised to know that a lot of these bands were very much in alternative music genres, rather than the musical theatre in which Collabro performs. For example, I started playing bass around this time and got quite heavily into bands such as the Red Hot Chili Peppers, Muse, Blink 182 – quite left-field compared to the music I am known for singing now. The Chili Peppers' 2002 album *By The Way* was one of my favourite albums and still is – the pop and slap bass on that is just incredible.

I started studying renowned bassists. An obvious starting point was Flea from the Chili Peppers, who is just the most incredible musician. Then I discovered Les Claypool of Primus, as well as people like Cass from Skunk Anansie (possibly my favourite band – I even have a tattoo on my foot quoting a lyric of theirs, 'God licks your face'). Initially I was heavily into funk bass and I practiced really hard. I thought I was getting quite good then one day this bloke who had been cleaning my dad's windows said he'd seen me playing and would I like to go round and jam with him? I went to meet up with him and he was unbelievable, I instantly realised that I pretty much knew nothing about playing bass! I learnt a lot from him.

After funk I started wandering around a whole range of musical genres. I am also really into orchestral music, especially for movies and games; I think I picked up that taste from a lot of the soundtracks for games like *Final Fantasy*. On a more extreme level, I don't know why I got into it but I have always been quite keen on hard metal, a lot of tech and grind core. I don't know where it started and where it came from, to be honest. Growing up, I think one of the first bands of that genre that I really loved listening to was Slipknot. Some of my friends were into them and I started buying the albums. They looked so extreme and the music was just like nothing else around at the time. I am naturally very curious about music, gaming, art, things like that, so as soon as I knew the Slipknot back-catalogue, I wanted to look further, investigate the bands that had influenced them, find out more similar music, discover more about these metal musicians and so on. The bands that are less in mainstream culture always fascinate me. Slipknot have had many imitators over the years but they genuinely paved the way for a whole new type of metal. Through researching the bands around Slipknot, I veered off into all sorts of interesting stuff, so I started to find albums by acts such as Pantera. Before I knew it I was quite heavily into some fairly extreme metal, and I became fascinated by the musicianship involved in songs that, to the outside ear, sound pretty hardcore and even confusing. A lot of metal is a series of rhythmic exercises so it sounds like a bit of a mess if you don't know what you are listening to and haven't heard a lot of it before, but actually it is so precise. Eventually you learn to listen to it and become accustomed to the songs' structures and then you realise it is amazing. These people are so talented to be able to memorise a seemingly random set of rhythms that might go on for five minutes.

I still love listening to these bands to this day. Groups such as The Arusha Accord, SikTh, After The Burial, these are all amazing bands. It didn't matter to me that the style of music was very different to the musical theatre I was often performing, there is a great skill across all the genres that you should always respect, even if the music itself isn't your thing. For example, the so-called 'screamo' bands might sound quite deafening to someone who isn't used to that extreme sound, but I researched these bands and discovered that the way the vocal cords work, or rather what is called your 'false' vocal cords, means that if they are correctly engaged, then it creates this overwhelming wall of sound when they scream. Bizarrely, the sound is the same for women as it is for men using that trick. This is the sort of thing that I find fascinating to discover and read up on. I find it all very interesting.

My love of metal also obviously influenced my own style, in terms of what I wear and also my piercings. At one point I had 15 piercings, but now I'm down to five. I have one through my septum in my nose, which I hide for photo shoots because I know that not everyone likes that look. I also have a micro-dermal in my back.

Perhaps not surprisingly there weren't many kids into those kinds of bands in Louth. You don't tend to hear After the Burial blaring out of a passing tractor. From the age of 14 I was really into all these bands with a few friends and when I was older and we started going to gigs in different parts of Lincolnshire we realised that there were loads more metalheads there. I think I started quite late with gigs. I'd been to those Slade shows and a few concerts with my dad, but my first gig with mates was Enter Shikari in Skegness. Their singles such as 'Sorry, You're Not A Winner' and 'Anything Can Happen In The Next Half Hour' are amazing but their albums are brilliant too. Those gigs were fantastic; they created so much energy in the room.

My mid-to-late teenage years were full of me playing in local bands. I won't list every band I was in because there were quite a few but suffice to say I loved rehearsing with my mates, writing our own material, putting the occasional little EP out ourselves – it was brilliant. My first notable band was just after I started learning to play the bass. I had a friend and she played guitar and my main friend in Louth had also started playing guitar too. So like loads of kids that age, we made a band and I sang and played bass. I don't think anyone else in the band could sing and I was known for being a singer so it was just kind of obvious that was my role. It was fun for a first project. We sat down and wrote lyrics and little bits of original music. We called ourselves Five Shots Left and thought we were amazing. But we weren't at all! We called our songs things like 'Sonic Death Monkey'. But hey, you have always got to start somewhere. Not exactly musical theatre though!

Then I went to sixth form in Louth, but I really didn't get on with that at all. For me, the tutors still treated us like children because they'd taught us since we were 12-years-old and even though they'd seen us grow up through our teens, their perception of us still seemed to be as young teenagers. I was doing drama, music, art and photography but I just didn't enjoy myself. The music part was good, but I just wasn't very good at photography. I enjoyed the drama and also did well at art. However my heart wasn't in it. Away from the sixth form I was doing my bands and also getting more and more into drama. When my grades started slipping after a year of that, I made the decision to get out of sixth form and enroll on a BTEC in Performing Arts at Lincoln College.

I was still living with my mum in Louth at this point. She was working at the time in a museum and gallery in Lincoln, so every day she would head into town and I would catch a lift and go to college. However, pretty soon it became obvious this wasn't going to be practical in the longer term because we were doing rehearsals and shows that might not finish until midnight sometimes, so I kind of bit the bullet and moved to Lincoln.

That was exciting, I was just 17 and I had to get my own

place. Looking back on it now, I haven't got a clue how I paid my rent. That first flat I got cheap with a friend because it was an interim period between people moving out and the new tenants moving in, so it was empty for a while. That was good fun but we had to move on, obviously; I did live in quite a few places and, if I am being totally honest with you... how can I put it?... maybe I was not exactly reliable with my rent. I was young and always struggling to find the money and perhaps inevitably I did get kicked out of a couple of places. So I moved around the city centre quite a lot, but to be honest I enjoyed that, I got to know all various parts of Lincoln. It's not a very big city; you can probably walk from one end to the other in an hour, so I enjoyed really knowing my way about.

When I started college I was still very much an introvert. I was in bands, doing gigs, I had some good friends and I would go on to appear in these various productions they put on as part of the course. However, I was still quite quiet. I wouldn't go out and just talk to people; I was still quiet and very laid-back. There were quite a lot of cliques and although I had my individual friends, I didn't seem to fit into any of the more popular cliques. Actually I made far more friends in the gigging scene, outside of education. Everybody was so friendly in the gigging scene whereas – perhaps obviously – in my drama course there was quite a lot of 'drama'. I guess that is to be expected when you have a lot of extrovert performers in one space, there is always going to be conflict. Big egos tend to clash. I am not really one for that kind of thing. If there is conflict I will distance myself from it rather than get involved in it. Some people can't wait for their next argument, it's almost like they need to have conflict to let their tension out, but that would just make me more tense. I had a great circle of friends from the gigging scene but there were also some great people at college who, like me, weren't interested in being part of the 'cool' cliques. So I settled in well and started to have a great time.

The college course was a BTEC qualification in performing arts. I did two years of that and it was a lot of fun. We did quite a few really cool productions, such as *Godspell*, in which I played Jesus, and *Tommy* where I was Captain Walker. I had a fun time there and I passed the course with a triple distinction. That obviously justified my decision to drop out of sixth form completely.

It wasn't just about the course either. That period was really enjoyable: socialising with new friends, discovering the city, going to gigs and clubs. Moving into Lincoln was great. In terms of music, there were obviously far more bands and more variety than in Louth, so I got to know lots of other metalheads and people who were really into their music. In fact, there was a huge following for metal in Lincoln, which was great, and there were some big local bands too.

I did struggle for money, which was perhaps inevitable. It kind of goes hand-in-hand with being young and starting to fund your own life. I had numerous casual jobs to try to make ends meet during this period. My first job was at the museum where my mum worked: there was a cafe there so I started doing that but I was late a few too many times and got the sack. I did some Christmas temping at Top Man and then worked for Lloyds shoes but I was late a few too many times... so I got the sack. Then I worked in a bar called The Annex but before you guess what happened next... I didn't get sacked from that job because they went bankrupt first! I turned up for work one day and they just said, 'Sorry, you haven't actually got a job any more.' I wouldn't mind but that was the first job I'd been on time for! I also worked in a pub but the landlady and I really didn't get on. One time I asked for Valentine's Day off but when it got round to doing the rota she put me down to work on Valentine's. When I asked her why she'd done that, as I'd specifically asked for the time off, she said, 'Well, you can take it or leave it.' So I left it.

This was also a very busy period in terms of bands I was playing in. Looking back, the variety of styles was ridiculous. I'd had a funk start, then I went through a rock phase; then I joined forces with a fellow music student in a 1980s hair metal band but with a modern twist; then I joined what was probably my main band – a group called Dirty As Muck.

If you had to generalise Dirty as Muck's style, I'd probably say we were indie rock. We actually did quite well in and around Lincoln; in fact, I think it's fair to say we were 'almost infamous' in the area, which was really nice. I played bass and did backing vocals (they already had an established singer when I joined). We did a couple of EPs that we released ourselves locally – all original material. Lincoln is quite small so you kind of get to know the local promoters and the people that put the gigs on. It was really good to be a part of that little scene.

We even had a few people follow us around. We had some great gigs and also some not so good ones! At one particular show, everything that could've gone wrong did. The guitarist managed to snap a couple of strings and then shortly after I somehow managed to break the thickest string on my bass, my E string. I still don't have a clue how I did that. Interestingly, because all the odds were stacked against us, we just went for it and actually it was a really good gig.

When I finished my BTEC, the rest of the band had another year of their course left and I didn't want to leave them marooned without a bass player, so I asked the head of music at the college if there was anything he could do to help. Brilliantly, he said he could put me on to the second year of a music course which meant he'd be able to grant me a qualification at the end of it. This meant I was able to stay in Lincoln, keep gigging and working with the band and have something to show for it in terms of a qualification at the end of the year. So I actually deferred starting university for a year because I wanted to stay with my band and it was the right decision because I really enjoyed my time doing what we were doing. Eventually after a full year of gigging, the band did kind of move away, only because we all went off to different universities, but it was a really good experience and I am very glad I was part of that. After Dirty As Muck I joined a metal band, so by then I had ticked off most genres of local bands!

I really enjoyed the rock and metal gig circuit in Lincoln. It's not really in my nature to go out clubbing; as you now know I am something of an introvert. I don't drink so to some degree my perfect night in would be on my own with games. I am not being antisocial in saying that; it is just that sometimes I prefer my own company. However, when I was in Lincoln I loved going to gigs and rock clubs. We were always really skint but there was this one particular club called the Sugarcubes where we used to go to that would be £1 to get in, then we would just dance for the whole night. We wouldn't buy any drinks – we'd just dance. Everyone went there and it was a really great place to hang out. I really enjoyed that period: great friends, good nights out, in and out of various bands, going to gigs – it was a brilliant time in my life.

Following the BTEC I started university aged 20. It wasn't really something that I had to think about because ever since I was a little kid my mum had said things like, 'I have a bank account and I am saving up some money for when you go to university,' so I just assumed that was my path: GCSEs, then sixth form, and then university. To be fair, that was always the route I wanted to take too.

I did some auditions and got accepted into the Thames Valley University (which is now known as the University of West London) to study an acting degree for musical theatre.

I knew a couple of people from the BTEC course who were at the same Uni so that helped me settle in quickly. Apart from that, I didn't make many friends in the first year, again because there were different cliques and a lot of personal drama that I didn't want to associate with or be around.

The course was fantastic. Apart from the obvious singing, acting, and dancing lessons, they taught us a lot about various elements of stagecraft. I remember one time we were shown all about stage fighting – how to punch someone realistically and yet safely and how to make the correct sounds. Another time we learnt all about sword fighting, it was really cool. The fact it was heavily practical suited me down to the ground.

In the second year, I moved into a new place and one day I bumped into a guy called Dicky on the street. I knew him from my course and it turned out he lived pretty much opposite my new flat, so we became good mates. He was a gamer too and, along with another friend called Max, we spent a lot of time gaming. Dicky had a bigger room in his place so we'd head over there and spend hours on *Super Smash Bros*. We became a comedy trio of sorts and it really worked for me in terms of being a little more out-going because Dicky was a comedian, unintentionally funny a lot of the time but really humorous, and Max was really witty as well, so it was hilarious being around them. I wasn't as quick on my feet with that kind of stuff so hanging out with them helped me with it a lot.

We were like the 'Three Musketeers'! Dicky and I used to call Max 'Harry', so we became known as Tom, Dick and Harry.

In the third year we all moved into the same house with another one of Max's friends, Adam. This guy was a music tech wizard who could do anything with an Apple Mac. We moved into this house and had a really good time. That's when I started going to the gym a lot. I don't know why Max and I decided to start but we were always very scrawny. I'd always been skinny, partly because I have a ridiculous metabolism. When I was 18 I only weighed nine stone and stayed at that weight until I was 22. So Max and I started going three times a week and pretty soon we were going religiously. I started at nine stone and just through working hard in the gym (I now go five times a week) I put on two stone. It's actually quite odd to get used to the feeling of being more muscular, when you've spent much of your life weighing only nine stone. On one occasion they did various tests at university to find out why my metabolism was so fast and found out that just standing still I burn 1,400 calories a day. So for me it's a case of not eating enough rather than eating too much! In fact now I have to take calorie supplements which are 1,200 calories on their own, just to stay at the same weight. I have wondered if this is all related to my IBS. I have been to see so many doctors but they can't find anything seriously wrong with me, even when I'm hunched over in pain in their surgeries, they can't find anything wrong. I've had x-rays, blood tests, dietary analyses... and nothing has ever come up. The things I know set it off are alcohol, caffeine, too much sugar and fizzy drinks. I also know that to a certain degree it is psychosomatic, because when I get nervous it goes off, but at other times I can be completely calm and it will still be there. So I lead quite a healthy lifestyle but it is only really half by choice; the other half is necessity.

TOM

In the third year of university, I was in a barber-shop quartet. Our friend Ben said he really wanted to start a group and we were all really excited by the prospect. We got some harmonies and songs together and we started performing at parties and such like. We would do songs such as 'Down by the Riverside' and 'Afternoon Delight', classic songs like that. Our most notable performance was at one of the screenings for the Olympic ceremonies, which was in front of a big crowd near Tower Bridge. We called ourselves Diplodicus Rage which we pronounced Di-PLOD-i-cus Rage! It was a really fun and enjoyable group to be a part of.

I decided around this time to adopt a stage name but it took such a long time to think of an alternative to my surname Leak. I had to send my card off to the actors' union, Equity, which checks if someone is already using a certain name and I was bugging my friends for ideas for months but nothing was coming up that appealed to us. Then one night we were in a theatre in Ealing having a drink after a show and I suddenly saw a sign on the wall that said, 'The Redgrave Room'. I said, 'That is it! I am fed up of thinking about it... Thomas J Redgrave.' It was only a few days later that I remembered about Vanessa Redgrave and her acting family, so no, I am not related to Vanessa!

In terms of my actual music career, things were about to look up. At one of the shows that the university produced, an agent was in the audience. He approached me afterwards and offered to take me on to his books. Soon after he said he'd got an audition for a job in a touring company going around schools in Italy, which sounded exciting. I went along and sang 'Strangers Like Me' taken from the soundtrack to the *Tarzan* animated movie. They liked it, and then said they wanted to call me back to sing something rockier. Given my background in metal bands, that was not a problem! I went back and sang 'It's My Life' by Bon Jovi, which they loved, so I got the job. That was a big moment because it was my first paid work.

Coincidentally, just before the Italy job came up, my friend Max had been offered an unpaid theatre adaptation of a classic Japanese movie piece, which from my personal point of view would have been fascinating. The film was called *Princess Mononoke* by a company called Studio Ghibli. I would've loved to have been involved in something like that but I needed the money so I opted for the Italy job.

We were due to be in Italy for six months, touring around theatres and secondary schools and putting on a musical version of *Hamlet* to the school kids. I played Horatio, Laertes and 'The Actor' and we rehearsed for three weeks. There was also a dance routine to learn, based on a Lady Gaga song, which was a challenge for me. It took me a little while to learn but once I had it in my head it was fine – I enjoyed it.

Following our rehearsals we went out to Italy. It was great fun but quite gruelling and exhausting at times. I wasn't sure at first about the language barrier but actually most of these kids spoke brilliant English. We were performing most days, certainly five or six locations a week, and the cast had to do all the background work too. So a typical day would consist of: get up around 5:30am, have breakfast, drive to the theatre or school where we were due to perform, unload the stage, rigging and lighting, set that all up, go and get into costume, perform the first show around 9am, then have a short break and do a second show around 11am. Then we'd take down the stage, load it back into the cars, then drive to the next location, book into a hotel for the night, grab some dinner, fall asleep, then wake up and do it all again the next day. We did that for six months, six days a week.

TOM

When I returned from Italy I had a nice lump sum of money sent to me by the touring company from a £50 per week retainer they'd kept back. That bought me some time to choose my next step. I lived off that for a little while then I started getting a bit low on money so I began looking for a job again. Luckily my girlfriend was working at a Japanese restaurant at the time and helped me get a job there. I really enjoyed that: I learned some of the culture and all about the different foods. I have always been very big into Japanese culture because of my gaming hobby: *Final Fantasy*, *The Legend of Zelda*, *Pokémon* – they were all created in Japan (I have never quite grown out of *Pokémon* – I still play!).

As a quick aside, you might think it seems a bit tenuous but I do think there is a link between my interest in musical theatre and my fascination with RPG games. Obviously the two things are poles apart, but what they do share is a common interest in great storylines. The whole point of musical theatre is telling a fantastic story through song and portraying emotions, and I think all the way through my life I have been drawn to any artistic field that tries to do the same. High quality RPG games do that as well.

Anyway, back to my own storyline! During this time I also performed in a pantomime with a company called Pyramid Pantomimes. We went around west London primary schools putting on this little production of *Aladdin*. Just like in Italy, it was all hands on deck – so I was Aladdin as well as the Sultan, and the girl who played Princess Jasmine also doubled as the elephant. We used to joke that she had to make sure she got her costume changes right otherwise I'd be professing my love for an elephant! That was a lot of fun; I was really lucky because I really got on with the people I was working with so it was really nice.

I auditioned for lots of jobs but didn't always get them. I

auditioned to be what is called a 'scarer' at Madame Tussaud's, but apparently I wasn't scary enough. I auditioned in a tutu and pink wig for a role in a drag group at Madame JoJo's. I didn't get that either. Perhaps the most unusual job I *did* get was a few sessions of life modelling. On one occasion I modelled for a student at Goldsmiths University. They sat me on a chair not wearing very much, apart from a mask that covered the whole of my head. The outside of the mask was covered in yellow fabric so you couldn't see my face at all. It didn't smell very nice and it wasn't particularly easy to breathe. I was perched on a stool facing this abstract art instalment, which was a rock with a picture of a person's face taped to it. Apparently it was all about seeing me as an object and the object as a person. We were meant to be 'staring' each other down in some kind of artistic face-off. I got into a particular position and then about 30 of the student's classmates and his tutor came in to the room and stood around me, discussing the art behind the 'piece' for about half an hour. It was actually really fun to do and very interesting to sit and hear them all talking about it. I wasn't self-conscious at all, not least because no one could even see my face. It was a fun way to earn a few quid to help with the rent – even just to earn a little bit of extra money to keep me going.

It was late in 2013 when I saw an advert on social media for a new boy band. Someone put a status up, friends were sharing it about and eventually it got to me. As much as I'd enjoyed all elements of musical theatre, at times I felt that my perfect job would be singing. I was still working at the Japanese restaurant and still auditioning for jobs, so I thought I might as well give this new band audition a go.

I put the date in my diary. *Who knows where this will lead?*

CHAPTER 4

MICHAEL

When I think back, one of my earliest memories is of my family all heading off in the car to do something nice and me sitting in the back singing along to one of my sister's CDs. For some reason, those car journeys really stick in my mind. I was really young, probably five or six, but I used to sing along to all the words. My sister Louise is four years older than me so she was pretty much in charge of the stereo and my first musical influences were led by what she liked. She used to listen to tons of pop music, including Take That, Boyzone and The Spice Girls – all those typical 1990s bands – and inevitably I would get into that. She could always remember every title of each song and which album it came from. I, on the other hand, could never remember the song title, but for some reason I could *always* remember the lyrics and the melody, almost straight away. So I'd be sitting in the back of the car singing along to a Boyzone song word-for-word, and if Mum asked me what it was called I'd say, 'I don't know!'

Mum says I was also really into 'Starlight Express' and would ask for that song every day but I don't remember. Having said that, as an adult I do love the show, so maybe she's telling the truth! I can pretty much remember the whole soundtrack off the top of my head, if I try. I guess from that point of view musical theatre has always been an important part of my life; it always seems to have been around to a greater or lesser degree – always there in the background. Mum's favourite musical was *Les Misérables* and she says that she used to play it to me in the car when I was a baby.

I'm very proud and fortunate to say that I had a very happy childhood. I couldn't have asked for a better upbringing. I grew up in Petersfield, between Guildford and Portsmouth. My first house was in a little cul-de-sac in a quiet little corner of town, and there was a big square of tarmac outside our house to play, which is where I remember learning to ride my bike, scooter, and play sports. It was a really safe area for us all to play. I had a really good set of friends in the cul-de-sac, who were all the same age as my sister and me. It's nice to have memories like that.

I have always been very close to my sister. I would actually say she's pretty much been my best friend all my life. I don't really recall a time when we were at each other's throats. When she was 18 and I was about 14, occasionally she would come home with her mates from a night out and I'd be there, this slightly annoying little brother, saying, 'So where have you been? Who did you go out with? Why did you go there? What was that like?' and I can see now that she was probably a bit fed up with that. But she never let on. She's just fantastic.

My parents met when they were both studying maths courses at Exeter University. My mum worked for IBM and my dad became qualified as a chartered accountant with a 'big four' partnership. He then joined a provincial practice and became a partner, although for some strange reason I remember him coming home one day and saying, 'If I had gone into double glazing, I would've done okay!' The things you remember as a kid! Then on holiday one year my parents met a family who lived just around the corner locally; it turned out they needed a new financial director so my dad ended up working for them in this really nice local family business and he has done so ever since. Mum stopped working when she had Louise but now we've grown up, Mum also works for that company in bookkeeping and accounts.

Apart from the singing in the car memory, it's funny what your mind recalls from when you were really young, isn't it? In the old house we used to have one of those openings between the kitchen and dining room, a serving hatch, and my mum used to play this tasting game, so she would get all these things like mustard and Marmite on spoons. Then she would blindfold us and we'd have to taste it. That was great fun. I won a baby photo competition, although I only remember the photo, not actually being there winning! I'd managed to get a bowl of porridge upside down on my head, and it was all running down over my little face.

For as long as I can remember I've always loved to perform. I loved the *feeling* of performing. Even before I was old enough to join any theatres or productions, I was 'performing' at home. For example, I've always been really into making compilations of all my family's home videos. I edit them down and if there's a big occasion for someone, a birthday or anniversary, I will often make a film for them. When I look back at some of these now, I'm nearly always bouncing around in front of the camera, performing, singing, and messing about. I enjoyed the attention in that way. I always assumed that everyone dreamt of being famous but now I know that not everyone does. When I was little I used to tell my parents every day that I was going to be a TV presenter or a singer. Obviously at such a young age, you dream of all sorts of jobs, but that was my main ambition.

I went to Langrish primary school in Stroud, outside Petersfield. I don't have many memories of my primary years. There is video footage of me at primary school in my very first performance. I was the narrator in *The Bad-tempered Ladybug* and I had to read out the entire book while everyone else acted it out. I do remember thinking, *Hang on, I've got to read this really long book while everyone else is involved in the actual show!* I was also Grumpy in *Snow White* (my sister played Snow White). They asked her who I should be and she said 'Grumpy!' When I walked on with a massive spade I had this huge grin on my face though, so everyone was laughing. That's one of my mum's favourite memories of me in theatre when I was really young.

I joined the Petersfield Youth Theatre (PYT) when I was only six. The first performance that I clearly remember being in was a show called *Smile*. It's essentially about the life of dancing showgirls. There are loads of great songs in the show and I really enjoyed it. I was Little Bob, this cheeky chappie character, and I seem to remember having my own dressing room. I thought that was because I was really important but actually it was because of chaperoning laws! I also recall being really pleased I'd been given the part. I had to walk out on stage with this little comic in my hand and then jump up on a box next to these twin boys who were a bit older than me. I don't remember any of my lines; I just remember that sequence I had to do. We performed at our local theatre that held about 300 people and when I walked out on stage I remember feeling like it was the biggest room in the entire world. It felt vast. I've been in there since as an adult, and it just seemed so much smaller. Two years later we were lucky enough to perform a song from *Smile* at the Royal Albert Hall, 4th May 1998, in aid of Cancer Research – the Duke of Gloucester attended and the cast sang 'Smile' with Michael Ball and I was standing right next to him!

There wasn't really any music or performing in my family, professionally. In fact, no one in my family has ever had anything to do with music! My sister can sing perfectly in tune but she has no confidence when it comes to performing. She was a really good dancer as a child, but she'd never want to come out front of stage.

I say there's no performing in the family, but by that I mean professionally. However my mum's dad used to entertain us on the piano. He could play any tune you asked for even though he couldn't read music. My dad also loves a bit of karaoke! He has also helped out with a few local amateur dramatics productions for charity and would sometimes get up on stage with a friend of his who sang. He was always nervous though, even when it was just a bit of fun with karaoke, but he would get up and sing. Most of the time it's a unique version of 'Hi Ho Silver Lining' or 'American Pie'. He likes to put on a good show! I think I've inherited that from him. I always sang around the house and things like that, but when I was 12 I entered a karaoke competition and won with my rendition of Robbie Williams' 'Angels'. I don't remember the performance but I do remember being very excited to have won. Nobody in my family really knows where my love for singing has come from.

Around that age I also entered a video tape of me singing into a junior version of the BBC show *Fame Academy* which was enjoying great ratings at the time. Carrie Grant, a celebrity vocal coach and very well respected singer in her own right, hosted the junior version. I sent in a video of me singing 'It's Not Unusual' by Tom Jones, and they aired that clip on the telly. At the time, Gareth Gates was very popular and I had my hair spiked up and gelled like he used to. Another famous talent show contestant called Darius was also doing well at the time and Carrie said I looked like Gareth but sang like Darius. Although they said some really nice things about me, I didn't manage to get through to the next round. In fact the person in my round who beat me went on to win the whole show. There was no live performing for me, they just showed my clip, but it was an exciting experience, nevertheless.

When it came to leaving primary school, my parents made the decision to send me to a private school nearby, called Churcher's College. My sister was already there and really enjoying herself so they felt it was the right decision to send me too. I have fantastic memories of that school, right from the word go. For my new intake there were a lot of new kids joining and I remember the school put on this barbecue to welcome us all and I had the best time, made loads of new friends and it just carried on from there.

My mum was obviously keen for me to settle in so she encouraged me to sign up to every school team there was! I had piano lessons, I tried a little bit of guitar, I was in every sports squad – it was mad. I can't blame my parents though, I wanted to do all this stuff, I was always busy. I don't know how I fitted it all in. When I first got a mobile phone, I used to message all of my friends at 8am on a Saturday asking them what we were doing that day, which sports we were going to play and where, but often I wouldn't hear back until 1pm. Then they would text me and say, 'I have been sleeping mate,' and I was like 'What? I've been up hours, let's do something!'

Another time, it was the start of the summer holidays and on the very first day I remember I wrote all the days of the holiday down and then I messaged everyone and started booking people in on certain days to play with. So one day I saw someone in the morning to play tennis, then I met someone else for lunch, then someone else in the afternoon and someone around teatime, then I'd stay overnight at someone else's.

I was very sporty and really competitive. My dad is very competitive and Louise too, so perhaps we get it from him. I was into pretty much any sport. My dad actually coached the rugby team so I used to do that plus I used to swim six times a week, even training before school some days. I got pretty good and eventually I represented my club in swimming galas and my rugby team were Hampshire champions. Swimming was probably my main sport but I also joined the teams for hockey, cricket, tennis – all sorts. I even won a couple of competitions at the local golf club where I was a member. When I was older, I was also part of the College Cadet Force (CCF). This was an after-school club run by the Army, Navy and RAF where you could go on these courses to gain knowledge in those professions. You could learn survival techniques, marching on parade, how to build bivouacs, how to stay afloat in a canoe, things like that. I went with the RAF and I remember being taken to an airfield and going up with a pilot who explained how the plane worked. They'd even do stuff like corkscrews and loop-the-loops; it was such a good opportunity, so exciting.

I was constantly on the go. I would be in the drama club at lunchtime then go and play for the first team at rugby, then go to some after-school club as well so I had a pretty varied set of friends! Sometimes some of the harder rugby lads would say, 'Oh, what are you singing and dancing for?' but then they wouldn't complain when the same fast footwork got us a try! As long as I was playing well, they didn't really mind. I certainly wasn't picked on or anything like that. I had to rush from one game to audition for *Oliver* still wearing my muddy kit.

I wasn't especially super-popular at school; I was just a normal kid. I wasn't in the cool crew but I knew everyone. There was a girl in the 'cool crowd' in her last year and I mentioned this one kid to her and she said, 'Is he even in my year?' I just couldn't believe that she'd been at school with someone for five years and didn't know even know them. Like most schools, there were a number of groupings. At my school it was pretty simple, the 'cool' crowd, the 'normal' kids and the 'geeks'. That's a really crass generalisation but it's also pretty accurate. I never understood why the cool kids would never speak to the geeks and vice versa. I just chatted with every one.

My parents always encouraged me in all of my teams, clubs and societies, so they'd drive me around to all these places, which was a lot of work for them. My mum is the most giving person – she will do anything for anyone. She used to help with the costumes at the local youth theatre and would work late into the night sewing and making costumes. She is so kind and helpful to people. If everyone volunteered like she does then it would be amazing. If I phoned her now and said I needed her to come to London, she'd jump in the car without even asking me why. She is amazing.

I do recall I had a little phase of thinking, *I'm quite good at everything, but not brilliant at anything.* Kind of like, 'the jack of all trades, master of none'. I noticed how I was never picked last but I was never chosen first either. I never felt like I was the best at anything. Mum just said it was great that I could play any sport with anybody and that in time whatever I really wanted to excel at would make itself known. That was just a phase and certainly now

MICHAEL

I am really grateful that I grew up playing so many different sports.

Our family holidays were also very hectic. We'd go on these trips abroad and while some families just chilled or sun-bathed by the pool all week, we'd be windsurfing, sailing, playing beach games, and water-skiing. Sometimes I wouldn't necessarily realise the opportunities that my parents were creating for me. Not in a selfish way, but just because I was a teenager and you don't always realise at that age how brilliant things might be. I'm embarrassed to say that one year I went on a school trip to the Grand Canyon and I was like, 'Oh, blimey, it's just this big hole in the ground, come ooon!' It's comical, but actually after we'd started hiking around I really got into it, then they took us up in a helicopter over the Canyon and I was like, 'This is the best thing ever!' My parents also took us to Australia, to the Great Barrier Reef, to New Zealand where we saw the *Lord of the Rings* film locations; we flew over New York in a helicopter, to Disney quite a few times – Orlando – it was just brilliant. Part of me wishes that I'd been a little bit older when I had some of these adventures because I think I would've appreciated them more. That said, I had a great time and fully appreciate how expensive it must've been and how adventurous my parents were for taking us. I am hugely grateful for all those amazing experiences we had as a family growing up. I was very lucky. Looking back, it was just fantastic because I was encouraged to have a go at everything. I couldn't have asked for a better childhood.

During my secondary school years I really got into amateur dramatics. The Petersfield Youth Theatre put on loads of great shows. Each year we would put on a show during the summer holidays, so, for example, *Bugsy Malone* was one of my favourites. We also did *West Side Story, Guys & Dolls,* shows like that. At this early stage, however, and unlike some of the other lads in the band, I never got the leading role. When I was really young I played the lead role part of Oliver Twist in *Oliver!* It was really cool to play the lead role even if it did mean hiding in a coffin on stage for a few scenes after singing 'Where Is Love?'! In my teens, though, I never landed the lead roles which was very disappointing. However I now understand that if you're not right for the part then that's the way it is and sometimes a cameo role is better than playing the lead. One of my favorite cameo roles was as the Cat in *Honk*. My parents always encouraged and supported me 100 per cent. No one ever told me, 'You are going to be famous', they would say things like, 'Michael, you always give it your best, or 'Michael, well done, you really lift everyone up, and you make them smile'. You know those end of year quizzes at school, where they have questions like, 'Who is going to be famous first?'? Well, that would never be me at this age. I was always 'Most likely to be a millionaire' perhaps because I was good at maths.

I still absolutely loved it. Rehearsing never felt like a chore to me. I couldn't get there quick enough. I was learning from some amazing people. The work that goes into putting on a show is phenomenal - from the programme, the set, lighting, sound, costumes, chaperones, musicians, choreographers and of course the director. The big yearly performance tended to be near the end of the summer holidays so we'd all work really hard in the lead up to that. Mind you, I didn't necessarily do loads of theatre outside of that summer holiday show, so musical theatre was often restricted to just that one month a year.

I feel very fortunate to be able to say I don't remember feeling unhappy as a kid. Not properly unhappy. I always had friends and always looked positively on everything. I was always just happy to be there; I think I just tried to be excited about things because the way I look at it, you never know when it's going to end. In fact, I'm smiling constantly writing about all of these lovely memories. I really hope that I can give that childhood to someone one day. I have been really lucky. At school they used to give out these awards at the end of each year and on more than one occasion I won the 'Biggest Smile' award. I'm very happy and lucky that that is the case.

Although I try to look positively on everything there are always hardships that children go through growing up and for me probably the most emotional and sad experience was when my mum's dad passed away from bowel cancer when I was 16. He was a brilliant grandad. He loved his gardening and he'd grow runner beans and let us help him pick them. He was in the RAF and he used to tell me all these amazing stories; he had really happy memories of his time in service. When he became ill, my mum didn't tell my sister and me how unwell he was because I was right in the middle of undertaking my GCSEs. I wasn't sure which college I wanted to go to, so I guess she was nervous about upsetting me and causing more problems with my studies. Then one morning she woke me up and said he'd passed away and I just turned on to my side and cried for the rest of the day. At first Louise and I were really upset with my mum for not telling us how ill he was, but I do realise now why she did that.

I enjoyed studying and I was fairly academic – at least I managed to get lots of A*s in my GCSEs anyway. When it came to choosing my A Levels, I really wanted to do drama, but I was also really good at maths. I guess when both your mum and dad work in finance that's probably going to be the case. I know it seems like an odd mix but I do like maths. I like sitting down and doing Sudoku.

Hey, don't judge, that's just what I like to do sometimes! I used to always win the maths prize every year. How sad! So, anyway, I wanted to do A Levels in maths, further maths, geography and drama – not your everyday selection! So I applied to Alton College and after my interview with them, I decided that actually I wanted to be a doctor, so I ended up studying maths, further maths, biology, chemistry and geography.

It was a brilliant school and we had some of the most amazing experiences. When I was 16, I was involved in a project called World Challenge. The basic idea was to raise some funds to fly out around the world and do charitable projects with some of your teachers. I had to raise quite a lot of money so I did cake sales, tombolas, sponsored walks, all sorts. We all managed to raise the money so we flew out to Thailand and headed for Bangkok. I remember on the very first day we landed I went to a local market and bought a Superman T-shirt for £1.50. I thought it was the best bargain ever but then the local guide told me I should've bartered! It was such a different culture. Rather daftly, on the first day I also bought a massive wooden elephant – because my sister had come home from her adventures with a wooden giraffe – but I didn't really think it through because then I had to spend the next six weeks trekking around Thailand with this bloody great wooden elephant under my arm! The teachers on the trip made each pupil a team leader at some point, and when it was your turn you had to allocate tasks, work out the food and money, and decide when the team had to do everything that needed to be done that day. We went trekking in the jungle, we walked all around Bangkok, went to an orphanage and school in Cambodia where we taught English to the children before seeing Angkor Wat and the amazing temples, then we finished off the trip with an amazing relaxation week living on a boat in Hanoi,

Vietnam. It was just the most incredible adventure. I had the time of my life.

I did some work experience with a career in medicine in mind but it didn't exactly go very well. The work experience with a GP was fine but then I was sent to work with a surgeon. Next thing I know, I'm in an operating theatre and they are performing a vasectomy. We had to shave this guy's privates and prep him for the operation. They'd given him his local anaesthetic and just as they were starting to cut him with the scalpel he yelped, 'Oooowwww!' I just saw this blood and heard that yelp. I was already on edge so at this point I nearly passed out. I turned away to catch my breath and calm down, and I found I was facing a mirrored window, which gave me an even more close-up grisly view! So I had to walk out. I came back later for another operation when they were removing some cancerous cells from someone's bladder, but I found the whole experience uncomfortable. They were experts, obviously, but just seeing the really physical way they had to man-handle people's bodies, it was really quite shocking and unforgiving. Not for me! That put me off forever. I can't even watch *Casualty* now!

If the work experience wasn't enough, I actually found biology quite hard work. There were people in my class who were naturals at it, they just understood how the body worked and it all came relatively easily to them. They'd get 95 per cent as an average mark but it felt much harder for me. So I started to think about a career in finance instead, obviously with my parents' experiences in my mind too. I got good grades and by then I'd decided I wanted to go into finance. I'd like to say it was all very focused and deliberate but I also remember the fact that 'Accounting & Finance' always came first in all the prospectuses I had for university! I applied to three universities and got offered places at all of them. In the end, I chose Bath to study Accounting & Finance, which was a four-year course with one of those years gaining experience in the industry.

I went straight to university after college – I didn't have a gap year. I hadn't been doing that much drama or musical theatre at this point because I'd not taken the A Level and then when I got to university I was too busy partying. One funny story is that I didn't drink alcohol until I was 18. I had a bet with my dad that I wouldn't drink alcohol until I was 21 and if I didn't he would give me £21,000. By the time I was 17, some of my mates were having a few beers at these little house parties and it was becoming quite tempting to party a bit more, like most kids of that age. After the first few parties, I remember talking to my dad and saying, 'Well, we've got our bet so I'm sticking to that, I will win that £21,000,' and he said,

'Hang on, I said £2,100!'

So I said, 'Stuff that!' and I went and had a beer! By the time I was at university all thoughts of winning that bet had long since gone out of the window. I did have my fair share of drunken student silliness, but in a way that's part of that whole period of your life, so I don't have any regrets about that. Besides I never did anything really bad. Plus, the sensible part of me tends to sober up really quickly if one of my mates is really drunk, so all of a sudden I am the level-headed one who makes sure no one gets hurt or falls over, and that everyone gets home safely.

Don't get me wrong – I hadn't suddenly turned into some drunken student bumming around. I was still really busy all the time; I was in all these societies, teams and clubs. University was just a continuation of my hectic secondary and sixth form life. I actually remember one good friend being a bit awkward around me for a few days and eventually I asked him what was the problem. 'You're just a bit too happy,' he said. 'We just want to relax and not do anything but you are always wanting to do stuff!'

It's funny looking back – I don't actually think that's a bad thing for someone to say about you. I didn't mind, anyway – I am not the type to hold grudges. I would hate to be in a room where I felt that someone didn't want to talk to me so I would never project that onto someone else. There's just no point.

It wasn't until the second year at Bath that a friend of mine was chatting with me about various shows we'd both been in previously and she said she was going to join the musical theatre society. She knew I liked performing and we'd had loads of fun at karaoke nights, but I'd not done anything in musical theatre at university. She convinced me to audition for the show *Footloose*, but I never expected anything to come of that. Then I was travelling home one weekend when I got a text from my friend. It just said, 'Now that's what I call a leading man!' I didn't know what she meant so I phoned her and that's when she told me I'd landed the lead role! Better still, she had won the leading female role, so we were going to be starring opposite each other.

We had the best time rehearsing for that show. It was such a nice group of people and I loved every second. It reignited my passion for performing and for musical theatre. You do hear all these horror stories of how people in musical theatre and the West End can be very competitive, but my experience of amateur dramatics and musical theatre is the exact opposite: I have always found people to be so lovely and friendly, it's a really supportive, amazing community that looks out for each other no matter what.

There is actually a video of the *Footloose* show. It was just the most fun. I'd made this entirely new set of friends across the university years and from different backgrounds too – it was brilliant. My whole family came to see the show, as always; they were so supportive. Watching the show back now I'm not entirely convinced it was as high a standard as we thought at the time, but we rehearsed so hard, we were a real team, I had a fantastic time and the audience loved it.

That year I was actually doing 12 months in industry too, so I started working at a very big international accountancy firm called PricewaterhouseCoopers. I felt like I was a very small fish in a *very* large pond, but everyone was really nice to me. Every few weeks you would get a review of your work and I frequently got reports saying, 'Michael is always on time, Michael is really fun to be around, Michael's very good with the clients,' which were obviously really nice comments. I really enjoyed meeting the clients and mixing with other members of staff and I feel like I have used these attributes to our advantage to make Collabro as successful as possible.

Dad was really helpful during my degree. Obviously the difficulty is a step up from A Level and sometimes I would come home from university and say, 'I don't understand this, Dad.' He would always understand it and he'd sit down with me and talk me through it. That was really lucky. I eventually came to learn basic accounting and tax and I really enjoyed working at the accountancy firm.

In my final year of university I auditioned for *Fame* and again I landed one of the lead roles. This time I was a dancer, which represented quite a challenge for me. I love to dance: my party tricks are 'The Worm' and walking on my hands. For this production, I had to learn one particularly complex dance routine and I really enjoyed the challenge. It's strange because if you put me in a nightclub I won't dance, I will just stand in the corner and talk to my friends, but if you need me to learn a dance routine for a show, I'm there. I seemed to be able to pick up the routines quite quickly and really enjoyed that production.

By this point in my degree and despite enjoying my year in the finance sector, I had made the decision not to pursue accountancy. During my year at the accountancy firm, I began a long-term qualification in chartered accountancy, but in my mind I wanted to push on with the musical theatre career. I was concerned that if I left a performing career too late it would scupper my chances, whereas with accountancy it is obviously a lot less time-sensitive. My parents were understandably keen for me to get the accountancy qualifications under my belt but I stuck to my guns and said I wanted to give the musical theatre a go first. The way I looked at it was that I could always come back to accountancy. Logically and pragmatically it made more sense to become a chartered accountant, but my heart was telling me something else.

So I decided to give myself a year with musical theatre, after which I would change paths again. I know I am strong enough in my own personality to say, 'Look, no matter how much you want this, it is not working. Time to move on.'

So I graduated and enrolled on a one-year post-graduate course at the London School of Musical Theatre, known as LSMT. Ultimately I went against my parents' wishes and paid the £15,000 annual fees for LSMT myself from the money I earned during the year at PricewaterhouseCoopers. The LSMT course was designed to teach you all these techniques and ideas about dancing, singing and acting. It was pretty intense and I just thought, *If I don't manage to make a career out of this after a year, then at least I will be far better trained at musical theatre.* The course was held in Borough in the Southbank area of London. I didn't have enough money to live in London and had to commute, but luckily the train from home took me straight to Waterloo, from where it was just a brief walk.

I had singing lessons for the first time at LSMT. I had the lessons in a group where you learnt warm-up techniques – how to hold your mouth, whether you move your shoulder in a certain way, your posture, all these little details. It wasn't just about technique; it was also all designed to make you more aesthetically pleasing to watch. There are so many minute details and little techniques you have to learn that are all a part of perfecting musical theatre.

At first I struggled a little with playing each character naturally. This was because I was so worried about getting the lines right that I didn't always fully immerse myself in the character. That's just due to a lack of experience and confidence. Eventually I began to understand what was involved and I started to really act. One particular role was playing a northerner who'd not eaten for a week. When it came to my performance I just lay on the floor in a wretched-looking ball feigning stomach cramps. I was spitting out my words in an exhausted, weary way, in a northern accent too and everyone was really complimentary about my performance. That was a real challenge because first of all I have a real sweet tooth so the notion of not eating for a week is horrifying to me, and secondly I didn't really know how to do a northern accent. Anyway, apparently it really worked so that was a big confidence boost. Without being overly dramatic, I'd say that was the first time that I thought, *Maybe I could do something with this...*

I loved the dance sessions at LSMT. People from the West End would come and teach us these really complex dance routines from shows, it was brilliant. I'm talking about performers from most of the big shows teaching us and you'd be sitting there chatting about dancing or singing with someone who at the time was appearing in *Les Misérables* every week.

That course at LSMT was really fun. I was singing, dancing and acting every day. I also made some amazing friends and, again, there was this little community of really nice people. Looking back, I can see that I have always enjoyed being a part of a team. Collabro is obviously the ultimate expression of that, but long before then I was always into my team sports. I enjoy the sense of community, people working together – whether that's rugby, swimming, or musical theatre.

I was surprised that people at LSMT were so friendly and community-minded. When you are doing amateur dramatics, the end goal is to put on a great show; it is not a commercial venture in terms of employment, so there's no competition for work. However, with LSMT, the ultimate aim was to get an agent and then be put forward for musicals in the West End, to get real paid work. Logically an agent is not going to take on everyone so I felt I had to be better than the others. So in a sense, we were all competing with each other for jobs. However, in my experience anyway, LSMT never felt like that; people were so lovely.

During this time I was still living at home and working at a petrol station. I had a series of casual jobs before then. When I was 16 I'd worked as a lifeguard at the local sports centre. I got free entry to the gym so that was really good. When I was at university I worked for Hollister, which I really enjoyed. Around this time I also applied to Next for a modelling competition and I got through to the top 50 but they wanted someone much taller. I love having my picture taken and I'm not ashamed to say that!

I was very nervous when it came to the end of the year at LSMT because various agents come into the school and see if they want to take any of the students onto their books.

There is a two-week window when all the agents come to see performances by the students. Usually you would sing a song first, then if the agent liked you they'd maybe ask you to do another song, or perhaps a monologue, or maybe some dance. The next thing that would would normally happen is you would get a text or phone call from the headmaster saying that the agent wants to see you again, this time for an interview.

I was getting nervous as the first week passed into the second and I hadn't yet been interviewed. Quite a few people I knew had already had interviews.

On the Monday of that second week, I had a bit of a moment with myself. I wouldn't say it was *the* turning point, nothing so dramatic, but it was definitely a moment when I faced up to what was in front of me and got myself prepared. As you now know, I have always loved performing but I actually didn't always believe in myself. I never *truly* thought I could do it. I never put myself forward to be a soloist. I never put myself forward to sing in a pub. There are people who go around saying, 'I am a singer, book me, listen to me!' At that point I didn't have enough confidence to be like that. I only sang at my sister's wedding because she asked me to. That was a great day on two levels: it was an amazing wedding and I got to see her and Jon become husband and wife, but also I am glad she asked me to sing because I have never really had an *unswerving* faith in myself like some performers do, and I think that is probably why I didn't get an agent in the first week at LSMT. In front of industry professionals like that you have to be, 'This is me, I am bloody good, sign me. You want to pick me, you will earn money through me.' However, I was walking into the audition room in that first week and my demeanour was more like, 'Hello, thanks for coming, I am a really nice person and I can sing in tune for you, please pick me because I am desperate'. That is not an attractive quality. For some reason, as that first week of agent auditions ended I finally recognised my problem, so on the second Monday I really steadied my nerves before I went in to perform. I thought, *Come on, Michael, get your act together, you need to get an agent... without fail.*

On the Monday I sang two songs to an agent and then did a monologue and to my delight, I received a message saying I had an interview. That was great news! This was the summer of 2013, and I said to myself, *If I haven't done anything worthwhile by June next year, if I have been struggling for money all that time and not making progress and don't feel I am good enough, then I will reconsider, I will re-evaluate.*

So to make some sort of breakthrough by June 2014 was the deadline I set myself.

Quite quickly I was put forward for a few auditions. The first one was for an adult pantomime which was essentially a risqué version of *Dick Whittington*. It wasn't really me though. I am not very coarse and I don't often swear; some people say I am a bit squeaky clean. The audition team told me I'd have to do a sex scene and therefore to come along with some similar dialogue, so I found a scene from a Jack Whitehall sketch where he was having sex and his mum was downstairs. I got through that and then I had to sing, but I started off way too high and made a hash of that. It was just a nightmare. Not surprisingly I didn't get the part. The next audition was to be an elf in a Christmas pantomime. When I got there another guy from LSMT was also auditioning and although I got down to the final two, ultimately he got the part. I hadn't exactly got off to a flying start.

COLLABRO

Heading into the winter of 2013 my deadline of June was fast approaching and so far I hadn't landed any roles. I was still working at the petrol station to make ends meet. I was determined to keep trying though. June was only a few months away.

Little did I know at the time, but my deadline to call it a day on the career in musical theatre would turn out to be the very same month that Collabro won *Britain's Got Talent!*

CHAPTER 5

RICHARD

My life has always been a balancing act between rugby and singing. I know that's an unusual combination, but those have always been my twin passions. My dad played rugby his whole life. After initially being quite a good footballer, he found rugby in his teens and just loved it. He ended up playing to quite a high standard and when he was working out in South Africa he joined a very good team out there. So rugby has been ever present in my life.

I wasn't actually massively interested in rugby when I was very young. Dad was one of the coaches of a local team and he'd always encourage me to play, but I wasn't that fussed at first. I remember there was this big industrial tube half-stuck in the muddy grass near one of the pitches and I just used to wander off the pitch and go and play with my mates inside it. We used to call it 'Teletubbyland', which didn't overly impress my dad when he was looking for me on the pitch!

However, as I went through my primary years, I got bigger and stronger and I started to really enjoy rugby. Even when I was only seven or eight, I was stocky for my age, so I would always play against the older kids. I started playing full contact rugby when I was only old enough to really be playing 'touch' rugby, the junior non-contact version of the game. Before I knew it, I *loved* playing rugby and that would be the start of a lifelong fascination with the sport.

Alongside my growing obsession with rugby, I was always encouraged to sing. My mum, in particular, is very musical. She was a chorister and loves to sing. As a girl she performed in a choir but then when her own kids came along it took a back seat. I don't remember her doing many public performances when I was growing up but I knew she could sing because she was always doing it around the house. Now she is getting back into it much more and has even joined a rock choir, which covers all sorts of contemporary rock songs. She loves that and it's great to see her finding the time to enjoy singing once again.

My dad was less of a singer himself – I'm not sure he could hold a tune in a bucket! (Only joking, love you, Dad!) – but he *loved* swing music and that has had a huge influence on me. He was also a big fan of opera, which has filtered down to me too. He would sometimes get up in the pub and belt out 'Cockles and Mussels' – so he has got it in him. The running joke in the family is that I get the melodies from my mum and the power from my dad. That is the balance, apparently, and it works for me!

At first I just enjoyed singing around the house or when I was out playing, although I wasn't in any groups or choirs. Every time we got in the car I would sing in the back and my dad tells me that I went through a phase of singing 'Barney the Dinosaur' constantly which probably drove him mad. On family holidays to Spain I would always sing at the talent shows. When I was four we were on holiday in Spain and the holiday reps had heard me sing 'Any Dream Will Do' from *Joseph* at the kid's club. There was a talent show on one of the nights and they asked me to get up on stage and perform in the show, but I didn't want to. I was petrified! I wasn't scared of singing; I was scared of the noise when the audience clapped – it was so loud! Hey, I was only four! In the end I asked the organisers if the audience would mind not clapping until *after* I had finished. They said they'd ask and so I went up on stage and did my little song. During the performance I actually faced the back of the stage. At the end, the crowd clapped wildly and I was so frightened I ran off stage crying! Despite this shyness, as I grew through my younger years I became increasingly fascinated with performing, as well as rugby.

I have very happy memories of my childhood home. I have a younger brother, James, and we were always really close, I love him so much. I have also got an older half-brother too, Alex, from my dad's previous relationship, although I don't see him as much as James because he is grown up and is married with a fantastic family (I go to visit quite a lot to see my gorgeous niece and nephew). We have a lot of love in our family, we are all really close. It was a busy house. Mum was a one-woman army rushing around – always making packed lunches, picking us up and taking us everywhere for school, clubs, teams – she was constantly on the go. My dad was originally an engineer before he was made redundant and became a taxi driver. I remember when I was 11 or so Dad was home on a working day during half-term and I just thought, *What are you doing here?* He was learning all the taxi routes, studying these hundreds of roads and maps. I actually remember him getting the call to say he had passed his taxi test, he was jumping all around the living room!

My parents used to take in student lodgers, which was always good fun. We had quite a few French students staying with us because Mum would take them in for a couple of weeks or so. Then she'd be even busier, rushing about making their meals and keeping the house clean and tidy, as well as looking after James and I. Sometimes there'd be as many as three students staying at the same time. For some reason I remember how she always used to set up the breakfast table for them before bed, I used to watch her doing that when I was very little, and she still does that today. She has so much energy! Having lodgers was fun as a kid – there were always fresh faces around and they had some interesting stories, and it was good for James and I to meet so many different characters from different parts of the world.

I was extremely lucky that my parents managed to put me through private education. I have no doubt that the local state schools were fantastic, but my only experience is of the private schools I went to. The opportunities they offered me were just incredible. I first went to St Christopher's school in Hove, which was a very well regarded prep school. My mum used to sing with one of the music teachers there, Michael Maine, so she'd heard how good it was. It was quite a small school – only about 200 kids from the ages of four to 13. It was set in this massive old house so it was very compact and super-friendly.

My mum and dad were not rich people. They certainly weren't able to easily pay for private education for James and I without noticing the cost. However, they really wanted to get us those opportunities and so they worked incredibly hard to fund our education. They worked *so* hard, and I just feel so lucky and proud of them that they did that for us. I remember going on a school skiing holiday when I was only ten and my parents had to pay extra but they somehow saved up over a few months and found the money. Mum didn't want me feeling left out from the other boys. To this day I have no idea how the financial pressures of funding our education actually affected them, but I do know they never stopped working. Mum cut corners and costs at home; Dad worked in the day as an engineer and did night shifts as a taxi driver. They never let on if they were under pressure; my home life was just so idyllic and enjoyable. My little brother and I have just the utmost respect for them – they are such amazing grafters.

Those primary school years were pretty good. I have generally happy memories but there were a few difficulties, if I am being honest. Like I said, I was quite stocky so I used to get a bit of verbal stick, people used to call me fat and that was quite difficult. I'm certainly not trying to make out I was bullied terribly – I wasn't – but I do remember people often picking on me for my weight. When you are that age and people say unkind things to you, it is hurtful and can really upset you. Despite my stature, I am quite a sensitive bloke and I couldn't understand why anyone would want to upset someone else, because I hate upsetting people or hurting their feelings. I take things very personally so that was quite hard at times.

When I grew a little older, however, I realised that my size – which was causing the problems – was actually the solution. I discovered that I was strong and had a natural power compared to some of the other boys. In one game, this kid had been playing dirty and he grabbed me and tried to pull me down off the ball but I wriggled free of him. I was really angry so I turned round to punch him in the face but he ducked down and I walloped my mate Harry straight on the nose! His gumshield flew out and he went down flat in comedy slow motion. It didn't feel very funny at the time and I'm pretty sure Harry wasn't very amused but we did laugh about it later. Another time I was playing rugby and there was a boy on my own team who kept saying nasty stuff about my weight, calling me fat, all that rubbish, and I'd just had enough, I was sick of it. At the time I'd been going to a few judo classes too, so when he said something nasty again I just grabbed him, flipped him up in the air and slammed him down on to the ground while shouting, 'Don't ever call me fat again!' He didn't. Neither did anyone else, funnily enough.

Aside from those nasty comments about my weight, I enjoyed primary school and had some good friends. We had a lot of fun. I remember one day we were in the playground kicking a football about and it went over the fence into the Jewish school next door. The rules said if the ball went over, you were supposed to go and get a teacher who would pop round next door and ask for it back properly. However, my mates egged me on to climb over the wall and retrieve the ball myself. I clambered up these slippery bricks, jumped down the other side, got the ball and then shot back up the wall to climb back into our playground... only to be met by Mr Sharpe, the history teacher, who was standing there frowning at me – my 'mates' had deliberately set me up and waited till I was over the other side before running to get the teacher!

I did a few school plays and productions during those early years, no real major roles of note, but I did enjoy my early forays into the world of performance. I did my first musical when I was nine with the Starlight Theatre Group, playing one of Gavroche's gang in *Les Misérables* (not the last time that production would have an impact on my life). That was amazing and a great way to start my performing career.

When I got to 13, I was due to move to a senior school, Hurstpierpoint College, which was also private. Unfortunately, the costs ramped up considerably so I know my parents had to work even harder. Luckily I got three scholarships which contributed towards my fees – for sports, music and drama. Ironically because I was trying to focus on all three areas, my grades sometimes suffered but without those scholarships I'm not sure how we could've afforded the fees.

The experiences we had at that school were incredible and they make me feel so lucky. We went on rugby tours to different countries, on theatre trips to the West End and we went to Stratford-upon-Avon to see some Shakespeare plays. The school just created the most brilliant opportunities for its pupils. I am not saying that everyone should go to private school – you should do what is right for you and your kids – but my parents felt that was right for us because of the opportunities we would be given. Those fantastic experiences really build your character. The school made that their mission – building well-balanced characters out of young people. Grades are great and the school was brilliant at that too, but in my experience Hurstpierpoint College was mostly about family and community. It was like this fantastic little bubble of people – all helping each other and being a real community.

One of my favourite school trips was when I went to California for a choir tour, which was just unbelievable. We travelled along the West Coast but I actually got very ill with streptococcus and my whole throat was in ribbons. I felt awful. I wasn't allowed to sing – which isn't great when you are on a choir tour – and they even suggested that I go home. There was no way I would do that though – I was out in California with all my friends on the trip of a lifetime! I was in this whole new country, which I never thought I would get to see – it was so cool. My parents had saved up for ages to pay for the trip and I stuck it out and had a brilliant time.

Rugby was still a complete obsession, in fact ever increasingly so. At 14 I'd been invited into the Harlequins Academy, one of the biggest teams in Europe. Even getting the trial for the academy was a big deal. There were about 30 kids asked to go along and try out, and I remember being very nervous. That was kind of like an audition, and to be honest it was the scariest thing. I felt as scared then as I would years later standing in front of Simon Cowell at the *Britain's Got Talent* auditions. A Harlequins rugby trial was a big deal – if you got into the academy you were among the ranks of one of the top teams and they would start training you and grooming you to become, ultimately, a professional rugby player. At that point it was easily the biggest moment in my young life and I was very nervous. Fortunately I got picked and they put me through to the academy squad, which was just the most amazing news. They had proper physios and coaches, the training was incredible, the staff was really experienced – it was superb!

That squad of young lads was really talented and as we grew through our teens we became an exceptional young group of rugby players. One of my fondest memories was winning the Sussex Cup twice in a row. The finals were held at Worthing Rugby Club – my dad's team – and all our school friends were allowed to come and cheer us on.

Due to my twin love of rugby and performing, I had two very different groups of friends. They were like two completely different worlds that didn't really go together. The idea of rugby becoming a career actually came earlier than singing. I would go through phases, especially over the summer when it was rugby pre-season and you don't play many games, and I would go through intense waves of singing, acting and performing. If I am being honest, acting was as much an ambition as singing was at that age and it remains a real passion of mine. I would love to appear in some straight plays or perform Shakespeare at the Globe Theatre – that would be a dream come true.

I performed in quite a few plays at Hurstpierpoint, which I absolutely loved. I appeared in *The History Boys,* and *The Importance of Being Earnest.* Even when I had a singing role, I always used to act for the songs anyway; I would always listen to the lyrics and bring the character into the song. I took some acting lessons and I also read up on the various acting techniques and theories, learning about the different methods of directing and acting. It was fascinating to me. I would like to think I take my passion for acting into my singing. It's not really that difficult to sing a particular song technically well, but the key is to bring some life to the person singing it, to become the character behind the words. You get to the point in professional musical theatre where everyone has a very similar level of technical ability, so it starts coming down to little things like the emotion behind the eyes, a small gesture here or a certain posture there. That's why I find musical theatre so fantastic, it allows me to combine my love of singing with my passion for acting.

Anyway, I'm jumping forward. Back when I was aged 16, I had done okay in my GCSEs, so the normal route would be to go to a sixth form college – in my case the one at the same school. However, this time my parents turned around to me and explained that they weren't sure they would be able to afford the fees. The costs had jumped up quite a lot to a really sizeable sum of money, but the scholarships stayed at the same level. I really wanted to go there – I didn't want to lose my friends and I didn't want to miss the new opportunities I knew I would be given. That said, I didn't want to see my parents making themselves ill from over-work, so I decided I would try and find the money myself. I was only 16 but I was determined to help my parents after all they had done for me. So in that summer holiday, when all my mates were out partying and having a great time, I started busking as much as I possibly could. I made up some backing tracks on my iPod and every spare minute I'd head into town and set up my little amp that I'd got for Christmas. I busked for hours, rain or shine, whatever the weather. I felt so driven, not only to get to the sixth form but also to make my own contribution. I never wanted my parents' efforts to be taken for granted and this was pretty much the only way I knew I could help.

I mostly busked swing music, which is my absolute favourite genre and a real passion for me. I sang Frank Sinatra, Michael Bublé, Nat King Cole and Ella Fitzgerald – I absolutely love them. Through putting in a *lot* of hours on the streets, I managed to busk my way to just over £5,000, which was pretty much the majority of my forthcoming school fees. I am really proud of doing that and at the same time I feel lucky that I could do it by busking, which I just loved. The school heard about my efforts and decided to help me with some of the costs. I was even featured on the local radio and in a newspaper, because people seemed to be really impressed by this 16-year-old kid trying to fund his education by working so hard. It didn't feel like work. I knew I was missing out on some partying with my mates but I was very focused on getting those fees paid for.

By the second half of my teenage years, I was very much focused on rugby. I was singing and performing in local productions and absolutely loved performing, but the rugby took precedence for a while. Although I loved both things equally, I felt that a career as a professional rugby player needed to happen when I was younger. It is a young man's game because of the fitness required and I felt that maybe I could pursue rugby and then turn to performing when the rugby career was petering out. Maybe that was being a bit idealistic, I don't know, but at that age you just want to think anything is possible.

One particular weekend I had a big rugby match and then in the evening I was appearing as Nanki-Poo in a production of *The Mikado*. Anyway, I got a bit of a battering in the match and my face was absolutely mashed up, bruised, swollen and cut. I had to get showered and changed and then dash over to the school to get made up for the show. It was comical – farcical really. There were times when I didn't know what I wanted to do first. *Do I go to more rehearsals or do I got to the match and risk getting hurt?* It often felt like a crossroads but I think rugby took precedence because of what I said about age.

I was playing a lot of rugby, training hard several times a week. I was getting bigger and bigger – eventually I was nearly two stone heavier than I am now, almost all of which was muscle. The position I played was prop and to succeed at a high level in that role you need to be big, strong and powerful.

At first the rugby was going really well but over time I started to get physical problems. I was training hard and I was strong and fit. However, during the Under 17s period, I started to suffer from chronic shin splints. The muscle was actually being pulled away from the bone and at times the pain was excruciating. This was exacerbated by a foot condition called plantar fasciitis, which is where ligaments in the foot become inflamed and can be very painful. The best way I can describe it is feeling like your feet are literally burning, like you are walking on hot coals. Training with these two conditions is not ideal but I was heavily into the rugby and so I just kept battling through all the pain.

The pain, however, started to become too great to even be able to run. The academy staff looked into my injury problems and tried correctional insoles for my heels. They tried everything – including all sorts of physiotherapy treatments. A few people reassured me that I would grow out of it. Unfortunately I didn't and the treatments just didn't work. I knew how to manage the pain to a certain point, but when you are playing at that high standard, you can't afford to miss a training session, not even once.

The combination of these two injuries had a massive impact on my game and soon I was unable to train on the pitch at all. I could still go to the gym and do all the fitness and conditioning work, but I wasn't playing enough competitive rugby. One week there was a huge event in Coventry where England selectors were going to be watching the youth teams, along with various scouts from professional clubs, as well as the main coaches of the academy. My parents and James came to support me and I was really excited, but in the back of my mind I knew my feet and shins were not right.

We did intense training for a few days and then they started to line up various matches. The training was painful enough but by the time I got to my first match my legs were just shot. I just couldn't run. I was devastated before I even started my first match. I was in peak physical condition, my cardio was fantastic, it was the best my body had ever been, and yet my feet and shins were letting me down. Once the match started, all my worst fears were realised. I would be on the pitch running but I just couldn't give any more because it was so painful. I had to keep stopping and eventually they took me off at half-time. The worst part was that because I didn't want to tell everyone that I had an injury, some of the coaches who didn't know me just thought it was because I was unfit. I was trying so hard, despite the horrendous pain. They didn't start me for the second game but said I would be subbed on, so I used a few painkillers and anti-inflammatory gels and thought to myself, *I have got to go on and prove I can do this*. When I was called up to play, I was all fired up but after about only five minutes I was in the most excruciating pain, so I literally had to sit down on the pitch. The pain was just so intense. I tried as hard as I could but my feet and shins were just in bits. So I sat down on the pitch and, as I did, I knew that this was the end of the road. Bear in mind this is in front of the best rugby scouts in the country. This had been my big chance to make it.

The coaches eventually took me to one side and said, 'Look, we are really sorry to say this, Richard, but your injuries are just not healing, we've tried everything but you are not even able to run in a match. It's just not working out.' They had been fantastic, to be fair, and had tried everything in their power to help me. I knew they were right; I just didn't want to admit that my potential rugby career was over. I had wanted it for so long and now it was just being snatched away.

I was absolutely devastated. In the car on the way back from Coventry, I actually broke down and cried – I was so gutted. I barely said a word. It was just a horrible day. I was only 18; I had just started committing to the idea that I was going to be a professional rugby player. Then suddenly, bang, it was all over.

After Coventry, there were a few days when I was just absolutely bombed out and gutted. It was made worse by the fact that there had been this massive build-up to the Coventry trials. Everyone locally knew about my big opportunity and was rooting for me, so all my friends were texting and phoning, asking how I'd got on, and I had to keep telling everyone I hadn't made it. My performing was going well but it wasn't at the same level as my rugby. I was still at college and I hadn't yet got any potential professional opportunities for my singing. So at that point, I just felt like my main career goal had been suddenly wrenched away from me.

I felt really sorry for myself for a few days then I just thought, *Right, come on, you've had your moan, you have been upset, what's happened has happened, you have got to deal with it, so let's move forward and focus on what you want to do with your life.* I'm not actually one to believe in fate particularly. I'm not an especially spiritual person but part of me did feel like something was telling me to concentrate on my singing career. So over the next few days I started to get excited about really focusing on my singing.

This was in the spring, coming to the end of the second term of sixth form, so we had A levels just around the corner. I have to be honest: I didn't get the best of grades, because I'd been committing a lot of my time to both rugby and performing. I do sometimes look back and think maybe I should've done a bit more work, but I was focused on the two things that I loved doing, which I saw as two very different but realistic career paths.

After the Coventry trials I sat down and thought about how I could improve my chances of making it as a singer. First off, I knew I needed to lose some weight – not fat, but I had a lot of muscle mass for rugby so I was quite wide. My size would've totally precluded me from getting a lot of roles, because it would've just looked wrong. So I worked on that and trained to slim down, losing two and a half stone. I really committed to the idea that I was going to go for West End work. I practised my singing non-stop, kept working on my physique, read up about musical theatre – I did anything I could to increase my chances of success.

I went from the beginning of the school term in 2011 believing I was going to be a professional rugby player then by the end of that year coming to the conclusion that I was going to be an actor/singer instead, and losing two and a half stone. That was a big year!

I was still busking and had started to get a little bit of a local following. Nothing major, but people would come up to me in the street and ask me to play at their wedding, or maybe an office function, that kind of thing. I started getting more and more gigs, which allowed me to earn a few more quid. It was great. Plus it allowed me to continue to strengthen my voice. People began asking if I had a business card or a website – of course, I had neither so I just got a Vistaprint card and website created, and began to feel like this little business was working okay. It wasn't like I had a big flashy website, it was pretty low-key, with my business card showing my details and a drawing of an old-school microphone as used by all my swing idols. I wasn't necessarily pushing it as this huge business aspiration but it was really enjoyable. My biggest gig was a wedding at Warwick Castle, which was just stunning. I think people liked the fact they had stumbled across me busking – it felt like they had made this little discovery, rather than going through the established agency networks for function singers.

In many ways I am not a natural attention-seeker. Let me explain: I love performing but not necessarily for the applause or adoration. I just really enjoy the actual performance and love seeing people enjoy that too, but I don't feel the need to get rapturous applause. It's nice when it comes but that level of admiration isn't the most important driving force behind why I perform. That's been the case for as long as I remember, right back from that time in Spain when I was a four-year-old and scared of the crowd clapping me.

That feeling still manifests itself when I am busking, although I don't tend to run off in tears anymore! What I love about busking is people coming up to me and saying, 'I really loved that song, thank you for singing it.' Or they might say, 'That was one of my dad's favourite songs, thank you.' Just lovely little comments like that mean far more than getting a load of applause. The fact I busk swing helps, in my opinion, because everyone loves swing music. There are so many well-loved classics, something for everyone. I used to sing Michael Bublé's 'Haven't Met You Yet' and one time a few ladies began dancing in the street. I swear maybe every two or three times I sang a certain song, such as 'My Way', one or two people would say, 'Thank you, that has really made my day'. Those comments are always really nice and so rewarding. That is what I love. Music makes people smile and makes people happy, and if I can contribute to that by singing to people then that makes my day too. Obviously I always wanted to sing to a professional standard and perform to huge audiences and entertain loads of people, but it has never really been about the attention, it has always been about making people happy and making myself happy.

I was now really focused on performing, looking for more formal opportunities. One of my last performances at Hurstpierpoint college was a production of *Anything Goes*, where I played Lord Evelyn Oakleigh. He is this Brit on board an American cruiser who falls in love with one of the showgirls on the boat. He is quite a comical character because he's very proper and goofy (for example, he suffers badly with seasickness). He has a fantastic song called 'Gypsy in Me', which I loved performing. The whole part was just really good fun to play. Luckily for me, there was an actor's agent at that performance and they approached me after my A levels and said they thought I could work well on their books. They said, 'Do you want to go for the West End?' and I was like, 'Yes, absolutely!' and so they took me on.

My first audition was actually for a very exciting film role – a part in *The World's End*, one of a famous trilogy of comedy blockbusters featuring the brilliant Simon Pegg. I was chuffed to even get the audition. That was a baptism of fire – I mean, I'd never even done a professional audition before! Just to be clear, I came straight out of college and never had any sort of training apart from maybe a few acting lessons at school and a few singing lessons. Before this I'd tended to always get the roles I auditioned for, mainly because I was one of the few guys at school who wanted to sing!

The film company required me to travel to London for the audition so I had to go out busking the week before to earn the train fare. The role was – ironically given my primary school situation – that of a bully. I was still quite big so they thought I would suit the role. When I got there, they asked me to basically act to this man behind the camera, so I did my thing, swearing and threatening this guy behind the camera. They seemed to like it so they said I would be called back and that this time I would be meeting Edgar Wright. He has always been one of my favourite directors. He's done all these amazingly creative films like *Shaun of the Dead*, so I was just over the moon to hear this.

For that second audition, I was so nervous that instead of acting to the person behind the camera, this time I acted into the lens. When I realised what I was doing I said 'Sorry, sorry, I'm just a bit overwhelmed, this is my first audition...' then I checked myself and thought, *What are you saying? Shut up!* Anyway they were really cool about it and asked me to try again. This time I acted as this bully to a woman behind the camera; I spat these swear words out at her and really got into the part. She actually looked quite scared! She even said, 'My God, you were horrible!' which I took as a compliment.

I was delighted when they phoned a few days later and said I had won the part. That was really exciting. I received the script on email and on the first day of filming I was picked up in a beautiful Rolls-Royce from the train station and driven to the set where I had my own trailer with my name on it. It was unbelievable. I really enjoyed the filming, obviously, and felt it was a real step up for me. Unfortunately, due to budgeting issues, my part was eventually cut right back in the editing room and ultimately I am only on screen for a very brief time, while the main character is having various flashbacks. I was obviously disappointed but there is not much you can do about it. Plus I knew it was good experience for my career.

I carried on pushing forward and started doing a few more auditions. I was up for a part in *Hollyoaks*, various local productions and other bits and pieces. I wasn't getting a lot, to be honest, and mostly I was still bumming around trying to make spare change to get the train up to London for an audition that I probably wouldn't even get.

One of the worst auditions I ever went for was a TV movie called *Robocroc*. In my opinion it didn't seem like a great idea; I thought, *Seriously, you have put me up for this?* The movie focused on a spaceship full of nano-robots that crash-landed into a zoo, releasing all these evil robots into the animal enclosures. Most of the robots find their way into a massive crocodile which transforms into a demented killing machine!

Anyway, I got the script and I personally thought it was awful, but I needed the work and the experience. I went up for the audition and as part of that they asked me to take my top off. It turned out that the zoo in the film was right next to a water park and there were supposed to be various people hanging around in their bikinis and trunks, just ripe for being eaten by this mad crocodile. When

I took my shirt off, they said, 'Oh well, you don't look like an 18-year-old guy, sorry,' and I was like, 'Great, thanks'. That has to be the worst role I was put up for.

People in the industry would often judge me before they got to know me or hear me perform. When I was playing rugby in my prime I was over 30lbs heavier than I am in Collabro. I would meet people and they would say, 'Oh, you look like a rugby player', and they'd just have this preconception of this heavy drinking, rough lad. Well, I can have fun, I like being a lad but I am also very sensitive and I enjoy being friendly and looking out for people. I love trusting people and I always like to think the best of people. However, when I was playing rugby, people would look at me and just assume I was this sports-mad knuckle-head. That used to get very demoralising.

Nevertheless, I kept on plugging away and then the opportunity came up to do *Miss Saigon* as an amateur regional production by the very prestigious Brighton Theatre Group, which is regarded by many as the number one theatre group for amateur dramatics in the country. There was an age limit of 19 on the actors for this particular production so my time was running out.

I got the role of John, one of the major parts, so I was delighted with that. When we were rehearsing, I got in touch with a brilliant actor called Peter Polycarpou because he'd previously done a workshop I attended and he was in the original *Miss Saigon* cast, playing John. I messaged him and said, 'You probably won't remember me but I went to one of your workshops and now I am playing John in *Miss Saigon*, it would be really fantastic if you could come along to watch and give us all some advice...' Amazingly, not only did he reply but he also came along and gave me pointers on my performance. How cool is that?

We performed *Miss Saigon* and then the company announced that they were doing *Les Misérables* for the next show. I just about had time before I turned 20, so I knew this was my last chance to play in that musical in terms of youth amateur dramatics. I love *Les Misérables*. It was the show that had got me into musical theatre; I had performed in it when I was just nine as my very first musical, I knew all the songs inside out, and I had grown up with that story. Now it appeared I would be performing in it for possibly the last time in a youth capacity, so it felt like it was meant to be. I liked the idea of starting and then finishing my young amateur dramatics career with that musical. There was a lot of money behind the production because the Brighton Theatre Group is pretty much top of the tree in that field. Therefore the venues were large, the sets were amazing, and it was a *very* big deal.

I landed the part of Valjean, the role that every male performer really wants. It was just the most amazing time, a brilliant production and I couldn't have wished for a better way to bring a close to my youth amateur dramatics career. The last night – 1st December 2013 – was actually my 20th birthday so I literally just made it!

By the Christmas of 2013, I was busking at least three times a week and doing a bit of labouring here and there when I was low on cash. I was getting pretty fed up; labouring was not what I wanted to do for a career. If I was really struggling for money and I couldn't get any labouring work, I would even go out busking in the rain. It was great to get the money and I still really enjoyed it, whether it was raining or not. My love of busking actually meant I got through a lot of rain-damaged equipment because I just didn't care, I just wanted to go and sing. Besides, the practicalities were that I had to make money to pay bills. I was living at Mum and

Dad's but I still had phone bills and other stuff to pay. I was pretty skint most of the time, to be honest.

I'd got my local gigs at weddings and the odd club night, plus the busking, but I still wanted to get myself out there. So I set up my own YouTube channel and started posting videos of me performing various songs on there. Again it was pretty low-key, I didn't have like a million subscribers or anything like that – just a few people who seemed to enjoy what I was doing. It was all very low-tech, usually just me in a dinner jacket and bow tie, sitting in my parents' living room and singing along to a backing track being played through my laptop. I don't have a great deal of knowledge of technology so it was all pretty basic stuff.

One time I decided to put out a post to see if people wanted to make requests for my next video. I had quite a few replies and several of them asked if I would perform 'Bring Him Home' from *Les Misérables*.

So I did.

I got the old dinner jacket and bow tie on again, sat in front of my laptop in the sitting room and recorded my own *a cappella* version of that classic song. It was the lowest budget performance ever. Then I posted it on YouTube and thought nothing more of it. Maybe some people would see it and enjoy it? Maybe they wouldn't.

At least it was out there.

I remember thinking to myself, *You never know who might see that...*

PART
TWO

CHAPTER 1

THE BEGINNING OF COLLABRO

MATT: As we all headed to the end of 2013, all five of us – separately – were feeling frustrated about our individual lack of progress. Speaking to the lads now, I know how much they all put in before Collabro even started and I completely understand the frustrations of going from one audition to another. It is hard to even get an audition, never mind go through and be selected. It can be very demoralising at times. However, it's your dream so you keep going until an opportunity opens up.

JAMIE: Couldn't agree more, Matt. I'd thoroughly enjoyed the holiday contract in Cyprus, I was beautifully tanned and feeling really good about myself; my voice was stronger than ever from all that performing and I was full of life. However even while we were still out there, my mind was always trying to think of what would be the next step. I am very driven and I couldn't let this ambition to perform professionally go. I have tried to let this go; I tried to go down a different route, learning Spanish, vocal coaching, teaching, but I always came back to singing. It just wouldn't go away.

MATT: As we mentioned, Jamie and I had bumped into each other on Facebook while we were doing those hotel contracts overseas. I'd heard Jamie's voice and was obviously really impressed; I thought, *Crikey, he's got a fantastic voice.* We got on well and had become good friends, partly because we just hit it off but also I think because of a shared determination to succeed.

JAMIE: There was a Facebook group for everyone working over there. I love Matt and always thought he was brilliant. We just clicked straight away. He has the same kind of awful sense of humour as me too, which helps. We had been talking for a while and we were both just sick of not getting into the West End, fed up of auditioning and not getting anywhere. I'd been auditioning for a few more years than Matt, so I was just really keen to make something happen. I know it might sound easy to say this with the benefit of hindsight, but I really do think if the work isn't coming to you, then you have to create your own. It is so easy to get disheartened by the process, but stop moping about and feeling sorry for yourself, just get out there and create your own work.

Whilst myself and Matt were working in Cyprus and Spain respectively performing musical theatre in hotels, the choreographer and the company we were working for had an idea about forming a musical theatre boy band. The choreographer discussed this at length with us as he knew how good we were to work with and our love for musical theatre drove us to get involved. The ambition was to look for work on the cruise ship and corporate circuits. That can be very lucrative and the standard of the performers is ridiculously high these days. To get a foothold in that world, any new band has to compete with the very best.

Their idea was that there just didn't seem any point in turning up in suits or dinner jackets. That's been done – it's been covered. Il Divo are the most obvious example: they are a phenomenal group and in terms of looking like that and having incredible voices, they have nailed it. I have loved Il Divo since their first album – my whole family has, especially my mum! – I have sung their songs at so many gigs and functions. So in my opinion, there was absolutely no point trying to replicate that.

So the choreographer and the company we were working for felt there was a gap in the market. People love musical theatre, they love *Les Mis, Phantom, Miss Saigon...* These shows have been selling tickets forever. Now it is starting to seep into popular culture, for example the *Les Misérables* film, and there are further adaptations on their way. Yet there wasn't a band that was young lads, dressed like normal young lads dress, singing musical theatre. It was a gap. There is a stigma around musical theatre that when you sing that style outside of the stage, you have to be either in character or smartly dressed. That needn't be the case. What Collabro is trying to do is make musical theatre more accessible. We are trying to carve out a new path and there are always going to be difficulties doing that, but then you have to be brave and just do it. Il Divo are incredible, and there are other great groups who dress more formally too, but back then there was a gap for something different.

MATT: So the choreographer and the company we were working for decided to stage some auditions in Kentish Town, north London towards the end of the year. In the interest of fairness, Jamie and I auditioned for the band because the new group needed to have the right members.

JAMIE: The audition room was pretty modest. It was just a basic rehearsal space. There was a piano and not much else. In that situation it is vital that you can hear the voices being auditioned very clearly. So we turned up on the day and waited to see the quality of the other people who were auditioning.

MICHAEL: It's really funny to think of you two waiting there while the rest of us gradually made our way over to sing with you. From my perspective, as I explained, I was heading towards Christmas and not really having any luck with auditions. I'd lost out at the *Dirty Dick Whittington* one and missed the part of the pantomime elf too. I was still putting in loads of shifts at the petrol station to keep the money coming in.

I said earlier that I wasn't entirely convinced the boy band route was for me, but something made me think I had to go along to this audition. So I made my way up to London for 10am, I turned up on time at what I can only describe as looking a bit like a derelict building! I was the first audition of the day. The people organising the auditions had asked us to prepare a mixture of musical theatre and pop, I guess to gauge our range and versatility. I went in there and sang two songs: 'Why God, Why?' from *Miss Saigon*, and Paolo Nutini's 'New Shoes'. Prior to my audition I chatted to this really quiet guy who was also there to try out for the group. This turned out to be Tom.

TOM: Jamie and Matt weren't having much luck back in England. I don't think any of us were at that point, to be frank. I'd seen the advert and it sounded like a really good idea to me, and something

I would really love to do. So after getting in touch I headed over to Kentish Town to meet them and audition. Obviously at this point the other lads were all complete strangers to me.

In my phone I still have the boys all listed as 'Jamie Musical Theatre Choir' and 'Matt Musical Theatre Choir', so that's what comes up when they call or text me. The reason for that is because when I read the original social media advert for the band audition, for some reason in my mind I automatically thought of a choir. I don't remember the actual wording of the advert but I just presumed it was a choir. I turned up and said, 'Hi, I am here to audition for the musical theatre choir.' They looked at me somewhat bemused!

MICHAEL: I have to be completely honest here and admit that I listened in on Tom's audition to hear how he compared. I'd chatted with Tom briefly. He seemed like such a lovely guy and I wanted him to do well. Then he came out and said he'd got a callback, so I was really pleased for him. At the same time, I was thinking, *Oh dear, that's one slot gone already...* Luckily they then came and told me they wanted me to perform again too. So Tom and I sat in the rehearsal rooms for about four hours while they listened to the other singers.

TOM: It was nice chatting with you while we waited, Michael. You never really know how these things are going to go, you either get the audition or you don't, but this was completely different because none of us really had a clue about what was going to happen. There was talk of doing corporate gigs and the cruise circuit, which can provide an amazing living, to be fair. I thought it would be good to sing with some new people and if anything developed from that then great, but if it didn't then so be it. However, as soon as I heard the others singing, it just sounded brilliant. By the afternoon they'd narrowed it down to ten lads, if I remember correctly, including Jamie and Matt obviously.

MICHAEL: Yes, I think that's about right. I had no idea how many people to expect when I first turned up, it could've been five or 55, so I was really pleased to make it through to the afternoon. I remember for the second round of performances, they mixed up two line-ups, chopping and changing the boys to see whose voices and harmonies gelled together best. This time they'd specifically requested that we all sang 'Bring Him Home' from *Les Misérables*.

JAMIE: I have very fond memories of that first audition, which was obviously the first time I'd met Michael and Tom. Myself and Matt knew that both Michael and Tom would be a perfect fit for the group. Michael is brilliant; he will do anything for anyone, so from the first audition he was the one that I clicked with the easiest. He was sitting in the corner wearing these white skinny jeans with quite long hair looking like this sort of posh Italian fop. Michael makes friends with absolutely everybody instantly. I am not like that, I tend to take my time and be quite selective, but he is friends with the world. When I first met Tom it was quite tricky to get to know him, because he is quite quiet and introverted. I thought he was really deep and philosophical, but actually he's mainly really geeky! Within a few weeks of meeting him, he'd converted me to all these games, plus Japanese anime, sci-fi and fantasy stories, so now I'm a secret geek and, therefore, we get on really well. Tom is kooky and really interesting.

MATT: Michael did seem very posh at first! He was so nice though, a real gentleman. Tom was quiet but you could see that he was a great guy and I kind of liked that he didn't turn up all loud and brash like some performers do.

TOM: After those second performances, the people organising the auditions broke the news to three of the hopefuls that they weren't progressing any further. Michael and I were still in though. They told us to go home and that they'd make their decision as quickly as possible and be in touch.

MATT: Tom and Michael sang amazingly well. To me it was really striking how good they sounded. By the end of that really long day auditioning, it was pretty clear that those two were going to be in the band. Jamie and me were also lined up too.

MICHAEL: About two weeks after I'd first auditioned I got a call to say I was in the group. I was in my room at home, it was in the afternoon, and the people who had organised the auditions just said, 'We really liked you and want you in the group,' and I was like, 'What?' Half of me was thinking, *I don't really know what this group is,* because there was no guarantee of any work or money, it was quite speculative in that sense. Yet the other half of me thought, *Yes! Finally, I have taken a leap of faith to do something with musical theatre and it might pay off.* I was still working at the petrol station so this was just really exciting.

They sent me a list of ten songs that they wanted me to learn, mostly musical theatre and pop. I've actually still got the list somewhere; I tend to keep mementos like that. They said, 'Go away and learn these songs, then come back in January when we will have a week's intensive rehearsing and then we'll see where we go from there.'

TOM: As I mentioned before, I'm quite laid-back about most things so when I got the call to say they wanted me in the band, I was obviously really pleased but I was also realistic about my expectations. I still didn't know what might happen with the band; we didn't yet have any contracts or work lined up, so it was brilliant but I didn't want to get too excited. Having said that, I was really grateful that they had given me the opportunity. I knew how good the other singers had been at the audition too, so it was clear that it was going to be very high quality performers I'd be working with.

JAMIE: With Matt and me also in the line-up, the band was almost complete. The chemistry with Tom, Michael, Matt and myself had been brilliant at the auditions in Kentish Town but the idea was always for the band to be a five-piece. So the people putting the band together decided that the solution was to scour the internet for a new person to audition.

MATT: Luckily, it was an absolute godsend because Richard popped up on YouTube singing 'Bring Him Home' beautifully. That was kind of like his audition really.

To think that it was just a slice of luck – for all of us – that he popped up on YouTube... amazing luck all round. Thinking about it, I guess if he'd posted a video with a different song or title for the listing, he might not have come to anyone's attention.

JAMIE: Richard said he lived in Brighton, which was close enough to London for us. We all needed to see him perform, obviously, even though the YouTube clips had already convinced us he had a brilliant voice. He looked right too. Richard was the last piece of the jigsaw and he fitted in even though he is a massive rugby lad! It really worked. It was brilliant.

RICHARD: I had no idea about the band that I was auditioning for, to be honest. I knew it was musical theatre. Actually I originally thought it was a musical theatre workshop, so I went along to see what was going on. I wasn't sure if I wanted to be in, so even as I was travelling up to London I still had doubts. I never saw myself in a band, to be honest. I remember going to meet the guys thinking, *Is this really what I want to do?*

Around this time, my girlfriend was doing a ski season in France so I went to visit her and said, 'I don't know if this band is right,' and she said, 'Just give it a go and see what happens.' I also spoke to a mate and he said the same – to give it a go. Of course, I look back now and it seems really silly, almost ungrateful, but you never know with these things. I never got my hopes up with auditions. Anyway, I went and met the guys, they were all really nice and it seemed to go well.

JAMIE: Richard clearly had a great voice and looked the part, but the people organising the band wanted us all to meet up and see if we would hit it off as personalities. Richard turned out to be a really stand out guy. He is a big team player and we were so fortunate to find him, and that voice, on YouTube. He sang for everyone and when we heard his voice it just all made sense. So they asked him to join the band. That was it, our five-piece. Taking our name from the notion of a collaboration of brothers, Collabro was christened.

RICHARD: When I found out I was in the band I was over the moon. I'd busked on the streets from the age of 16 for hours on end in front of loads of random people with no breakthroughs, yet I post a two-minute video on YouTube and this happens. How ironic. It just shows how the world has changed. I have since done a few school talks back at home and I say to the kids 'If you are interested in performing, put yourself on every social media channel you can think of, because you never know who is watching. You play a gig in front of 100 people and you might get some interest, but put your video up on the internet and there's suddenly millions of people watching your performance'.

MICHAEL: Next thing I know I get a text saying there is a new member of the band, this guy from Brighton, and that we were all going to meet up in January to start rehearsals. Soon after, Richard sent me a message introducing himself and we started chatting over texts.

JAMIE: I remember waking up in the New Year and wondering what was going to happen in the next twelve months...

MICHAEL: Over the festive period I worked really hard at the petrol garage, earned some money and enjoyed a really nice Christmas. Then in the second week of January I headed into London for the new band rehearsals at a pub.

Originally we were told we were all going to have to sing solos, to see whose voice had what sound. I was the most nervous I'd ever been because I was really worried I was going to sing again and they'd say, 'Oh, we're not sure now, you're not in the group any more.'

Richard was actually the first to arrive. I'd only ever spoken to him on text, I'd never seen him in person before. We started talking and then the other boys arrived. Then we were told that we weren't going to sing solos but instead we were going to crack straight on as a group.

RICHARD: Matt and Jamie obviously knew each other and they were good because they clearly tried not to be all cliquey and 'best buddies'; they made a real effort to make us all feel welcome. My initial thoughts were, *If this works out, these guys are going to become my best friends.*

TOM: I felt that with Jamie and Matt too. For me, as a quiet guy, when two people are that close and you come into their world from the outside, it can be kind of nerve-wracking, but everyone was really welcoming.

MATT: We all arrived at this pub called The Miller in London Bridge. We were obviously quite nervous, anxious to see if this new band would work. Apart from Jamie and me no one knew each other at this point, so it was a big day. Everyone met in the pub and shook hands, introduced ourselves and then headed upstairs to the rehearsal space to start working together.

JAMIE: You say rehearsal 'space', but it was pretty tiny! There was virtually no money to pay for anything bigger so we'd booked this little room above The Miller, which they used for occasional events. The Miller is a lovely pub and the people who ran it were wonderful, but this rehearsal space upstairs had no windows and it was all black walls like a little nightclub. There were builders in working at the time so for most of the rehearsals all we could hear was construction noise…

MICHAEL: ...and because there were black walls with barely any lighting and no windows, you didn't know what time of day it was...

JAMIE: ...Plus the floor was sticky with stale beer, so it smelt like a nightclub even in the daytime.

MICHAEL: Granted, it wasn't the most upmarket space but at that point, none of us really cared. Like Jamie says, the people who ran it were lovely and we were all just really focused on rehearsing together, seeing if there was something special about this new band.

JAMIE: Absolutely. Every day we would come into the same smell, the same dingy room, the same building noise – but you know what? None of that mattered. As soon as I met up with all the lads together I just had a feeling...

MATT: The first song we ever performed together as a five-piece was, you might not be surprised to hear, 'Bring Him Home'. I don't want to sound overly dramatic here, but the chemistry was incredible, it just felt *special*. Perhaps the cheesiest way to describe it is to make an analogy with *The Jersey Boys*. There is a moment in that story when those four guys are standing under a street lamp singing someone else's songs – effectively that is what we were doing. Then the Jersey Boys sing these harmonies, it all clicks and they look at each other and realise they have something special. For me, that is *exactly* how I felt when we sang 'Bring Him Home' for the first time at The Miller. The harmonies just worked, it was so natural. There were loads of different levels of harmony, all sorts going on in the vocals and yet somehow it just all came together to make what I now know is *our* sound. I don't know if the other lads agree, but for me that specific moment was amazing, really amazing.

JAMIE: Yes! It just fitted. I knew. I think it was a really amazing moment, I can't even tell you. I knew that it was special and I've never had that feeling before. Richard slotted in beautifully and it felt really good. We sang through a few other numbers and people's nerves started to settle down; we all started to relax. By then I just knew it was going to work. I can't explain this feeling that I had, but I just knew.

TOM: There was the moment and we all looked at each other. It sounded really good, it is always hard to say this without sounding big-headed, but it immediately felt like the band could appeal to a bigger audience rather than corporate gigs or cruise ships.

RICHARD: I thought, *We have got something different here, this could be something good.* Tom's right. It felt *big*.

MICHAEL: Totally. I remember thinking, *This could be amazing, I really want to be in this group, I don't really know where it is going or what it is doing but I want to be a part of this.* I could still work and earn money at the petrol station, then come and do this for fun, so I just thought, *Who knows, something might come out of this.*

TOM: Then we took a break for some lunch and sat around eating a few sandwiches and just chatting. Considering we were mostly complete strangers, we got on really well straight away. I'm not usually instantly at ease with new faces but I found the boys to be really nice and easy to talk to. It felt really comfortable.

MICHAEL: As that first week of rehearsals progressed, we started to realise that we could be really good friends as well as band-mates. Richard and I were still living at home, so they put us two in this twin room in a hotel during that week. We were rehearsing for eight or nine hours a day then going back to this hotel room together, so by the end of the week we were really good mates!

We spent four or five days rehearsing what worked and what didn't, learning around ten songs and it became clear to everyone involved in those early days of the band that musical theatre was the style that really suited the combination of our voices.

RICHARD: I quickly got very close to Michael because we stayed in the same hotel room. He is very easy to get on with. He worries a lot, but he is so on the ball, he just wants to make sure everything is sorted out. Jamie is the same, they are both very organised and logical, and they plan ahead. If the band didn't have them I have no idea how things would happen!

MATT: By the end of the week, there was pretty much a set-list collated together. Like we said earlier, The Miller was a fairly Spartan location, we worked very long hours and it was pretty tiring but that time just flew by. It was so exciting every time we sang together.

JAMIE: I should point out that around the time of these rehearsals, both Matt and I got offered fantastic cruise line jobs which were really well paid and would allow us to travel all over the world. It is rare, in our industry, to be offered anything as amazing as that, and when you are offered something like it, you take it. The job offer came from a lady called Belinda King, who is a giant of the cruise ship circuit. She works with all the top liners around the world and is hugely revered. I was offered the chance to take over the lead male from a guy called Lewis who would become known for doing extremely well in Andrew Lloyd Webber's televised search for Joseph. I was offered quite a lot of money and also a vocal coaching position on the ship too. And I turned it down... because I just had a feeling about this new band. That was a completely illogical thing to do: there was no security with this band, save for the agreements with the choreography/holiday company, we had no money in the bank as a group from performing, nothing at all. We all had to take a week off our jobs to even go to these rehearsals. Yet my heart was telling me to pursue this new band. Matt did the same with a similar cruise job and I think that tells you how good we sounded and how natural the band instantly felt. So we both turned down those amazing cruise ship opportunities.

RICHARD: When we were above this pub rehearsing, I remember my dad saying, 'When are you going to get a job, Richard?' I was travelling back and forth to London every day and staying in the hotel. It was really difficult, both financially and in terms of the long hours I was working. I had been out busking loads, just trying to earn some money to help pay for things. It was all pretty tenuous really.

MICHAEL: A few family members came up to the rehearsals and we performed for them, which in a sense was Collabro's first ever 'gig'. I also told some of my theatre friends that I'd been asked to join a five-piece boy band and they were not so supportive. A couple of them were like, 'Oh God, good luck with that, that's not going anywhere. I've got a West End audition...'

RICHARD: We all became close during that week. For example, the first time I went for a drink with Michael was after one of those rehearsals at The Miller and we ended up going to an Italian restaurant called Giuseppe's near London Bridge. They had karaoke on and we'd been drinking, so we got the backing tracks up and started singing to the whole restaurant in two-part harmony. We received loads of applause and in fact the manager came up to us afterwards and said, 'You guys should come back, that was brilliant! People want to know, are you in a boy band?'

TOM: The rehearsals went very well and by the end of the week we had all bonded and there were some really tight friendships forming. I thought about the next step: *Where is this going, how are we going to make this into an actual job that we can live off?* A lot of groups get together and do free gig after free gig for publicity, but never ultimately earn any money. With my job at the Japanese restaurant I was working so hard but only just paying rent, so I didn't have a lot of room for not earning. On the other hand I just thought, *What would I rather be doing, do I take a chance and go for it with this band knowing that nothing is guaranteed? Or do I just turn my back on this opportunity and go back to working in a job that isn't really my dream?* There was no contest.

JAMIE: There was just something about the band, the line-up, the personalities involved and certainly the vocal chemistry. The boys will attest to this: one evening we were all sitting together chatting and I said, 'Guys, 2014 is the year.'

CHAPTER 2

THE FIRST *BRITAIN'S GOT TALENT* AUDITION

JAMIE: It was a very exciting time. We carried on rehearsing and getting to know each other musically and personally. It was also very tiring because we were all still working loads of hours to keep some money coming in and I was still working three jobs – in the NHS, as a vocal coach and teaching Spanish. I used to wander around the supermarket or the shops and just be worrying about paying my rent for the next month. The money situation was perilous for all of us.

MATT: The very first show we performed as Collabro was a music industry showcase at Blackpool Pleasure Beach called 'Keeping It Live At The Pleasure Beach'. It was in this beautiful, big room with all these ornate balconies and an amazing stage, the sound just echoed through the place, it was brilliant. We knew it was a big deal. This was a well-regarded event where loads of agents from around the country went to see a variety of acts perform, ostensibly to see if they wanted to take them on and start representing them.

A lot of these agents could get us work in the corporate world or on cruises.

MICHAEL: It was a really interesting night. There were all sorts of performers: Jessie J tribute acts, dancers, magicians, groups – it was really varied. From our point of view we were still finding our feet in terms of what market we would sit in. Each act was allowed ten minutes so we didn't know whether to perform shorter songs with a bit of chat in between to show off our personalities or just do three songs. I was apprehensive because it was a tough audience, wall-to-wall with agents. We did 'The Prayer' by Celine Dion and Andrea Bocelli, Gary Barlow's 'Let Me Go' and 'Somewhere' from *West Side Story* – so a good mix. It was fun.

TOM: It was great fun. That was the very first time we had ever performed in front of anyone (other than our families) and we simply didn't know how it was going to go down. We did those three songs and, incredibly, we got a standing ovation! Remember, this isn't an audience who were there to have a good time; they were there to scout employable acts in a purely professional capacity. So it was a real shock when everyone stood up.

MATT: I couldn't agree more – it was a total shock. We talked before we went on stage and the feeling had been just, *This is the beginning of Collabro, start as we mean to go on, let's go out there and knock their socks off!* And that's what we did – we were the only act to get a standing ovation. The first time we'd ever sung together in public and we got a standing ovation. Although individually we had all performed for years, and no doubt got standing ovations as soloists or as part of a production, in terms of this band we were new to this. It was fantastic! What a first gig.

JAMIE: That performance was so enjoyable. We raised the roof! The odds were against us, really; we were sort of finding our feet a bit, which is only natural when a band starts. However, even though we sang a mix of pop and musical theatre, it went down a storm. I've been told that we went down in the history of that place because we were the first act to get a standing ovation. If that's true then I am really proud of that.

TOM: Yes, that was amazing when we heard about the standing ovation...

JAMIE: ...so we went on a big night out afterwards to celebrate. That was great because we had a brilliant time. We were still getting to know each other really. We were proud, excited and optimistic, all at once.

RICHARD: I think even as early as Blackpool the group was gelling so well.

TOM: This sounds *really* cheesy but I'm going to say it anyway: when you are rehearsing for days on end with people, standing in a group, harmonising, working through songs, putting in so many hours, then you go and stand on a stage in front of hundreds of strangers – in this case potentially very hard-nosed industry professionals – it does create a bond within the group. This is the cheesy part but I did warn you – you grow closer through song! It's true!

JAMIE: It is true, good point. You are thrust together into quite intense experiences and those sorts of performances really cement that bond.

Around this time, Michael was living with me on my sofa, Richard was travelling up and down from Brighton and the rest of us were in London. At our rehearsal rooms in Shepherd's Bush there were a pair of drum skins that had been signed by all these famous musicians and performers. I felt so good about Collabro, that feeling that 2014 was going to be our year, that I joked – only half-joking if I am being perfectly honest – that we should sign one of the drum skins too! I don't mean that to sound cocky, I just really, *really* felt positive about our prospects.

MATT: Like Jamie says, I had taken the big decision to move down from Carlisle to London. That was a risk. It's not cheap living in London and – with the benefit of hindsight – if either the showcase or the *Britain's Got Talent* auditions hadn't come off, I'd have been stuck for money very quickly indeed.

Luckily, this is when the Collabro story really starts to ramp up. Around the time of the Blackpool showcase, everyone involved at that stage discussed entering for *Britain's Got Talent*. When the idea was first mentioned, we thought, *What have we got to lose?*

TOM: I'd never thought of auditioning for *Britain's Got Talent* or *The X Factor* as a solo musical theatre singer. I didn't know how well that idea would go down on those shows. The good thing about being in a group is that there is something special when harmonies come together, something charming about five guys being so close and sounding so natural and in unison. If you are out there singing on your own, you are really vulnerable and that is why I have so much respect for all of the acts that did get up on stage alone. They are vulnerable and it takes a lot of guts and confidence. I can't imagine being up there on my own without the other four guys backing me up every step of the way.

Jumping ahead in the story a little bit now, but much later, when we were in the *Britain's Got Talent* semi-finals, a lot of keyboard warriors took to Twitter to say, 'There are too many singers in *Britain's Got Talent*, why didn't you go on *The X Factor?*' However, we felt that particular show wouldn't accept a musical theatre group, so we needed to go to a show that welcomed variety. That's why we went for *Britain's Got Talent*.

JAMIE: Absolutely. We felt as a band that our vocals were capable of appealing to a big audience, so the decision was made to send a video of us performing to the producers at *Britain's Got Talent*. They got back to us and said they liked what we were doing and asked if we would come along to audition. That was great news.

RICHARD: Then, on the night in Blackpool when we got the standing ovation, a few people approached us and said they were representatives of *Britain's Got Talent* and asked if we would be interested in auditioning for it. We explained that we'd already sent our video in and that it had got a positive response and they were really pleased for us.

TOM: We were given a date for our *Britain's Got Talent* audition and that was that: our second ever performance was going to be on 13th February 2014 at the Hammersmith Apollo in front of Simon Cowell, Amanda Holden, Alesha Dixon, David Walliams and 3,500 people.

MICHAEL: As soon as we were given the date for the audition we decided we needed more rehearsals – and fast. We were already very tight but the way this band works is that there is always room for improvement and we never rest on our laurels. Singing musical theatre with five-piece harmonies can be very complex so you really do have to put the hours in.

The rehearsals went really well. The plan was to perform 'Bring Him Home', the song that we'd first sung together at The Miller. It was a song that meant a lot to all of us and it seemed the most obvious choice.

MATT: During the week leading up to the first *Britain's Got Talent* audition, we had what I still regard as one of my favourite Collabro moments. Our own rehearsals were going well. Then at one point, I think about three days before the show…?

MICHAEL: Yes, three days before…

MATT: …Right, okay, that late on then, we decided to have a go at singing 'Stars', also from *Les Misérables*. 'Stars' is a very powerful song from start to finish so we were really keen to perform that. At this point we had moved into a room at the Dance Attic rehearsal studios in Fulham. We stood around a piano, the parts for 'Stars' were dished out, we learnt the harmonies individually and then we sang it. And WOW! BOOM! What a moment. It sounded incredible. I was like, '*This* is the song, this is the one; we *have* to do "Stars"'.

RICHARD: Everyone agreed: it was just perfect for us. Even though it was late in the week and we'd been working on other songs in the lead up to this, there was just something magical about the way

'Stars' sounded. 'Bring Him Home' was really good but 'Stars' was like, wow! I just really felt it.

JAMIE: The song just had everything that we needed for the audition. It had big sweeping parts and then it calmed back down and of course there was a big finale. It just screamed '*Britain's Got Talent* audition' to us. We loved it and we hoped that the *Britain's Got Talent* audience would love it too.

MICHAEL: I'd spent the whole week before *Britain's Got Talent* with Richard and I'm sure he will tell you he was the most anxious about appearing on the show. He was worried the programme might make a mockery of us. Don't forget, what we were trying to do had never been done before: a boy band dressed like we were, singing musical theatre. It was a risk. Richard was really concerned about that. We all were to a degree.

RICHARD: Michael's absolutely right, I was very anxious about that. To be fair, we had absolutely no idea whether people would like us, whether the show would portray us nicely. Maybe they'd think we were a joke act – no one knew. Obviously we thought we sounded good but there was no way we could say we were definitely going to go down well with the judges or the audience.

MATT: Personally I think it was a massive risk going on the show. As Michael and Jamie have said, what Collabro was trying to do had never been done before. However, once you put yourself up for that audition, that's the game you are playing. Like Tom said earlier, it was a pretty big leap going from a few hundred people at Blackpool Pleasure Beach to *Britain's Got Talent*, the Apollo and

Simon Cowell. I was anxious but I also felt we were ready; we'd rehearsed, the songs sounded great, and I was up for it.

We had to wake up really early to get to Hammersmith. I don't think any of us slept that much because we were so excited. We were probably overpowered by nerves too. We turned up together at Hammersmith to find everybody already queueing outside and I just thought, *This is crazy*.

RICHARD: It was the day before Valentine's Day – 13th February 2014. There is a picture of us all outside the venue waiting to go in for the performance and we all have our arms around each other. There are people queueing behind us and there is even a guy photo-bombing us in the picture!

TOM: At the time of that first audition, I was living in a big, old house with lots of cold windows, a lot of mould in there too, so I had to keep wiping vinegar on the walls to clean off the mould every time it started appearing. I was always trying to keep warm which wasn't ideal preparation for the audition. On the morning of the Hammersmith audition, the nerves still hadn't kicked in for me. Even when we met up at the venue, the nerves didn't start. I don't really get nervous until I am really near a performance.

I had watched a lot of *The X Factor* when I was younger but I hadn't seen so much of *Britain's Got Talent*. That said, I was aware of the past winners, and also people like Susan Boyle, obviously. I liked the fact we went for *Britain's Got Talent* instead of *The X Factor* and that reassured me on the first audition day.

MICHAEL: As you may have seen from the audition footage, we just wore casual clothes – jeans and T-shirts. We wore suits and jackets at Blackpool but afterwards we'd all said how uncomfortable we felt. Tom hates wearing shirts and ties. Even now when we dress up smart he will wear a grandad collar or a T-shirt with a blazer.

MICHAEL: None of us walk around every day wearing a suit so it just didn't make sense, if we were being true to our characters, to suddenly put these really formal suits on. Besides, we wanted to be different, as Jamie said earlier. Collabro's view was simple: we are five young men who want to sing a genre of music that is not stereotypically what young boy bands sing. By the same token, we didn't want to wear what musical theatre groups typically wear, namely formal clothing. So we just went in our own clothes.

JAMIE: Although I hated my shoes.

TOM: Have you seen my hair? I didn't actually have the money for a haircut at that time so I just have this big mop of hair.

JAMIE: We went inside the venue and were bundled into a room with hundreds of other acts and told to wait. Little did we know that it was just the start of a very, *very* long day.

MATT: It was a very long day, about 13 hours. From the minute you get in there, you go into the waiting room and get yourself sorted, get prepared, warm-up and immediately the cameras start. They stick microphones on you and begin interviewing the band.

RICHARD: We went backstage to do a little bit of filming and they filmed us chatting to another band and then we had to go and do a soundcheck. We didn't actually get to see many auditions but we were around quite a few soundchecks. We'd been listening in to a lot of acts soundchecking, to see what our competition was, and there were loads of really good singers who were getting good applause from the production team. Occasionally, however, we'd watch someone sing that we felt was really good and afterwards there'd be like one man clapping slowly out of politeness. It was all very tense. I thought, *Oh my God, I hope that's not gonna be us.*

As we were soundchecking 'Stars', a few members of the crew scurried past busily. However, when a good few of them heard what we were singing they stopped dead in their tracks, then turned and listened to the rest of the song. When we'd finished, loads of people clapped. That made me feel really good, I thought we might be on to something.

MICHAEL: To give you an idea of the time frame, I think the first soundcheck was about 10am but we eventually went on stage late in the evening. 'Stars' went down really well with the crew, like Richard said, but then the production team asked us what else we had got. We were trying to read into that, thinking, *Are they trying to help us or not? Is this a good sign or a bad one?* So we sang through 'The Prayer' by Celine Dion and Andrea Bocelli.

TOM: Normally when you're waiting for a standard audition you occupy yourself with thinking solely about the performance. However, for *Britain's Got Talent* there is so much other stuff going on. We tried to focus on the song; we went through it over and over again. I was still feeling reasonably calm but then someone said, 'What if we get buzzed in the first few notes of the song?' I hadn't really thought about that, and I think that's when the nerves started kicking in.

RICHARD: I remember there was a boy band who were getting loads of filming attention and we were like, 'Is that a bad sign for us? They have filmed them loads more than us...' The whole time you are trying to second-guess what's happening. Actually, everyone got treated the same, it was just that in our heads we were on the look-out for any sign of encouragement.

JAMIE: The 12 or 13 hours between the first soundcheck and the performance were pretty terrifying! There was so much adrenalin and it was all spread out over such a long period. It was a real balancing act to stay in control of the nerves.

MATT: Even though it was a long day, we were all just really fired up. All the filming kind of helped; it sort of takes over from the actual performance so you're not concentrating on your nerves. Then, finally, we were into the evening and someone came over to us and said, 'Right, lads. You are up next!' We all thought, *Brilliant, let's do this!*

RICHARD: I don't mind saying at times the whole day was massively overwhelming. By now we were absolutely shattered but the adrenalin was still there and when I heard the words, 'Collabro, you're up next', *it was pumping.* They walked us over to meet Ant and Dec – which is a really weird moment in itself – then they film our spontaneous reactions by the side of the stage and then that's it, we walk out to our big moment on *Britain's Got Talent.*

MATT: There was a shot of us looking through the curtain and you can just see Simon – for me personally, that is the exact moment when the nerves hit. It had been such a hectic day, arriving, meeting other acts, soundchecking, make-up, prep, all the filming and tons of interviews. Somehow, and I know this sounds daft, I'd almost forgotten about the judges being there. So when I peeped through the curtain and saw Simon sitting there and waiting to hear us sing, it was like being hit by a truck. That was the first time we'd seen him on the day. I thought, *Oh my God, look lads, it's Simon Cowell!*

MICHAEL: Plus there were an awful lot of people out there in the audience! The Hammersmith audition was the biggest audience that we sang in front of for the whole of *Britain's Got Talent*.

RICHARD: So they gave us the nod to start and we lined up in order and walked on stage. Suddenly the judges were *right there*. They are so unbelievably close to the performers, so much closer than it looks on TV. I remember thinking, *This isn't real, they look like I'm watching them on some life-size TV*. In fact they all looked so perfect, so manicured, it looked like high definition television. We've all said since that they were so perfect they were almost like waxworks.

JAMIE: Richard's right. Suddenly you have Simon Cowell sitting in front of you, larger than life, one of the most powerful and influential people in the world of music. We had no idea what he was going to say or do. It was just so surreal.

TOM: You see these four famous faces on TV and in the newspapers and they are so removed from your everyday life that when you go out there and walk on stage it is still like there is a television screen between you and them. Like Richard says, the judges were like waxwork models – it was not quite real. It just didn't feel like we were actually standing in front of them. For me, that kind of helped with the nerves because a little bit of distance was created and in a strange way it relaxed me.

MICHAEL: I have watched *The X Factor* ever since it started, as well as *Britain's Got Talent* and all the reality and talent shows. I think I have watched probably more of these shows than anyone else in the band. So to suddenly find myself on the stage was a very odd moment. Exhilarating, scary and bizarre all at once. When we came out we were obviously really nervous, but whenever I sing with these boys, I can't be that nervous because I know they are going to do an amazing job. For my part, as long as I just do what I know I have practised, I feel I will be okay.

MATT: We stood in front of the judges and I said, 'Hi there, we are Collabro.' We were all nervous, trying to make a good first impression. Then Alesha asked us our day jobs and we went along the line... labourer, sales assistant on a petrol garage, kitchen salesman, worker in a Japanese restaurant and finally Jamie, who said he worked in a hospital.

TOM: There must have been some Japanese in the audience because when I said about my job I got a little cheer!

JAMIE: That was all fine but when Alesha asked us how long we'd been together and Richard replied, 'About a month,' Simon Cowell rolled his eyes. This is not the reaction you want before you've even started to sing. Especially not from Simon, of all the judges. David Walliams was looking a bit unsure as well. Amanda I couldn't read and Alesha was friendly but actually deceptively grilling us!

She was really doubtful as to whether or not we were going to be able to perform anything worthwhile. I think she was just a bit sick of seeing boy bands all day. Then she said, 'What makes you think that after a month you are good enough to win *Britain's Got Talent?*' To which Matt replied, 'Natural chemistry, I think.' Good answer. Mind you, that's when Amanda puts her hand to her face and looks down. Again it was hard to read but I was wondering if the early signs weren't good.

MATT: The bottom line is, if Simon Cowell doesn't like you, forget about it, and I don't mind admitting that when Simon rolled his eyes I was terrified. I was just thinking, *I can see you are not sure, but please… just let us sing.*

RICHARD: For my part, when Simon rolled his eyes, the stocky kid from primary school in me felt like I was being pre-judged all over again. Simon's reaction wasn't anything to do with my size, I know that, but the judges and the audience saw us dressed casually, saying we were a boy band and they made a snap judgement. That's fair enough actually, but it does show you that sometimes those superficial appearances are not entirely accurate.

JAMIE: I was gutted when he rolled his eyes, but I also felt like Matt, I was just thinking, *Okay, I get that, but have a listen to this…*

TOM: I've got to be honest and admit I was oblivious to it, I didn't see him do that. That actually helped because if I had seen it that might have sown a seed of doubt in my mind. When Alesha said, 'A month?' that didn't really bother me either, because like I said, I am laid-back plus I had faith in the boys and the work we'd put in.

I just felt, *Nothing that they say is going to change how we perform or what we have worked on up to this point.*

Mostly though, I didn't actually agree that a month was a short period of time to be rehearsing. From the experience I'd had before this audition of doing jobs like *Hamlet* in Italy, three weeks was perfectly acceptable. We were only singing one song, after all. I think for Italy we'd three weeks' rehearsal for an hour-long show. When I was doing pantomime, which was only about a half an hour show for children, we rehearsed that in just three days. In musical theatre, you are expected to know all your lines, your harmonies, and your cues – that's your job. We had learnt the song, we came in knowing how we wanted to sing it, and we were prepared. So those comments didn't really faze me.

RICHARD: Those first few moments talking to the judges were really hard. These people can make or break your career. We had an absolute grilling: the producers don't show you the full edit but they were really asking us a ton of questions. After the filming Jamie said to me that it felt as if Simon 'was looking into my soul'!

While I was listening to all of this chat back and forth, my leg was shaking. I get this thing where my leg just buckles and gives way if I am really nervous. I get it at big performances. I usually manage to control it but I can tell you on that day it was shaking like mad.

MICHAEL: At this point I patted Matt on the back, as much to reassure myself as him!

RICHARD: Then I did the same to you...

JAMIE: Meanwhile I'm just standing there with my arms out straight, rigidly pointing down with fists clenched. That's my nervous stance. We were all standing in a horseshoe formation, so we could take some comfort from each other.

MICHAEL: Richard was preparing himself to sing the opening line. It's a big part to take on and I think it's fair to say that this is something he's become most well known for. That was a big ask.

RICHARD: I remember it being a complete blur. My leg was shaking away, I was really concentrating on my composure; it was really daunting.

MICHAEL: It is so funny watching the clip back and seeing Richard without a beard! I think that is the only day he's ever shaved.

TOM: We were all clean-shaven because we wanted to present a certain boyish image.

MICHAEL: While Richard was trying to stop his leg buckling, I was wiping my hands on my leg – that's how my nerves manifested themselves. I don't remember a lot about the actual performance, to be honest.

JAMIE: Then David Walliams and Alesha swap bemused glances when the backing track starts…

MICHAEL: The backing track is just our own karaoke version – it's not exactly high-tech.

MATT: Richard's opening line must have been difficult; it was, after

Little Jamie poses for
the camera.

8-year-old Jamie.

Jamie and his mum and sister, Lorraine and Caytee.

Matt shows off his dance moves.

Matt discovered his love of music at an early age.

Matt performs to 1,000 people in his first gig.

Tom as a boy.

Tom and his mum.

Tom in one of his many bands.

Michael having fun at breakfast time.

Michael takes part in one of his first productions.

Michael does a bit of modelling in the days before Collabro.

Richard celebrates his
first Christmas.

Richard pulls a face during one
of his first productions.

Richard and his dad on the last day of college at Hurstpierpoint.

Ready, steady, go! The boys have some fun on a photo shoot...

...Before getting down to the serious business.

Jamie, Matt, Tom, Michael and Richard pose for the camera.

all, the country's first impression of us. This was Collabro's first moment. This was it.

RICHARD: Wasn't bricking it at all!

JAMIE: Five words into Richard's opening line, when he's only sung, 'There, out in the darkness,' Simon raises his eyebrows again, but this time in a good way. He was really surprised. All of them were. There were a few cheers from the audience and you could visibly see Richard starting to relax, he turned towards the rest of us and sang the rest of his lines.

Then it was my opening line. You can tell I was nervous because that is not how I sing! But it went well and I started to relax.

MATT: That's when the harmonies started and also because of Jamie's voice you could tell the crowd were thinking, *Hang on, the first guy could really sing, now this guy can too!* Throughout the early part of the song, I was thinking, *Have we won them over yet?* The backing track was so quiet but I think it made it better for us because we could hear the harmonies more.

MICHAEL: The backing track was so low in the mix, I could barely hear it, so I heard those first cheers but they drowned out the backing track even more!

TOM: Then we all came in on the line, 'And if they fall as Lucifer fell...' and it really started to ramp up – the crowd were really getting into it. Simon began to smile slightly and Amanda began to look really emotional.

MATT: I was trying my best to look into the judges' eyes but it was quite intimidating. After that it was my solo, which felt quite long at the time!

TOM: I was looking straight out into the audience; I didn't clock the judges at all. That was deliberate: I grew up doing amateur dramatics and I have always been told to play to the back of the room. You don't want to be performing to the front rows only and leave everyone else feeling left out, so it just naturally came to me to perform to the whole auditorium.

RICHARD: I could see some of the front rows clapping but it was darker at the back so I couldn't see much more.

MATT: Once you get the audience reacting like they did – starting to cheer, clap and stand up – then obviously you know it is going well. The audience were loving the performance and the judges appeared to be too – so we naturally became more confident. I looked to Michael and Richard as I finished my solo. You can see throughout the performance – and this is still the case to this day – we look at each other quite a lot because we feel more together as a group when we do that. I guess it's just a reassurance thing. It's like we are telling each other how it's going; it's communication.

RICHARD: Matt's absolutely right. For example, after my solo, I remember looking at Jamie as if to say, 'Go on, mate, you can do this.'

JAMIE: When we sing together we take comfort. By the time we got to the small interlude, the crowd was clapping pretty wildly and the judges looked really moved; we knew it was going well. But we still had the big finale to nail so there was no room for complacency. I didn't look at the judges once all the way through. By now I was starting to really enjoy it... but you still don't know what the judges will say.

MICHAEL: I came in slightly late for my solo, but hopefully you would never know.

MATT: Probably my favourite Collabro moment is the walk forward on 'safe behind bars'. Everyone was loving it by now – Michael's solo had gone down really well – then we walked forward and this was the pivotal moment for me. Pretty much all of the audience started standing up and clapping.

RICHARD: We planned our walk forward; we thought we had to do something and in a way we knew it was a little bit cheesy, a typical boy band thing to do, but actually it just hit home with everyone. Then the three lads in the centre moved their arms in unison, while Jamie and I didn't, and that lifted it up another notch. By now it was going brilliantly. It wasn't a perfect performance by any means. A few of us missed our timings and I certainly forgot my harmonies at one point – you can see it in the footage clearly, I am just singing along and don't hide it very well. No one seemed to notice though.

MICHAEL: When we walked forward I almost forgot to move! We only decided to move on that part of the song about five minutes before we went on stage, to give it an extra something, so I almost forgot.
JAMIE: When I watch the footage back, it's quite an odd feeling because in my memory it is all pretty much a blur.

MICHAEL: I'm the same, to be honest. I can't remember where I was looking, I can picture the venue and the people in the crowd, and I can picture the reaction at the end but I can't quite picture anything else.

JAMIE: As we reached the finale, singing, 'This I swear by the stars', first Amanda, then Alesha and then David rose for a standing ovation...

MICHAEL: I saw the other three stand up and I thought, *Come on Simon, come on, Simon...*

JAMIE: ...Then, quite literally as we ring out the last breath of the last note, Simon stood up too. That was just an amazing moment.

TOM: You might be surprised to hear that I was so focused on performing correctly right until the end that I didn't notice the judges standing up until we'd finished the song. Then I looked down at them and I thought, *Oh, they're giving us a standing ovation!*

MATT: That was the best feeling ever! I was just thinking, *Oh my God, Simon Cowell is standing up.* We were obviously keen to see the other judges respond well but for Simon to be standing on his feet was a massive moment for us – the biggest compliment you can get. I had to fight back the tears; I was just so emotional – all of us were. This was the result of grafting and grafting and trying to get somewhere. People think you go on shows like *Britain's Got Talent* and instantly you are famous, but we had all worked so hard for a moment like that.

JAMIE: You can see from the footage that I couldn't believe it, I just completely broke down because so much work had gone into that moment – not just the rehearsals that week, not the long days we'd done at The Miller pub, not the months before that, but for all of us the *years* leading up to this one moment. I was overwhelmed – I literally couldn't even speak. I was so overwhelmed I thought I was going to collapse. I had spent my life waiting for an opportunity like that. It is really difficult, sitting there at home watching these TV shows thinking, *I can do that, why have I not been picked up, why isn't it happening for me?* Then suddenly here was Simon Cowell, one of the biggest music moguls in the world, giving us a standing ovation for something that we did. That is something to be really proud of.

RICHARD: When all the judges stood up, I remember grabbing Michael next to me and I was like, 'Yes! Mate this is sick, this is crazy!' I was just so happy. Then I noticed Jamie crying and I thought, *Why is he crying?* but obviously he was crying with happiness because he was so overwhelmed. It was a really intense experience.

MATT: The judges' comments were all really amazing. Amanda admitted she'd been crying and then said, 'I could just burst with pride for you because that was bloody brilliant, absolutely.' That was actually one of our goals for the performance, to make Amanda cry! So then it was Simon Cowell's turn to talk, which we were obviously very anxious to hear. He said it was an 'absolutely brilliant audition'. This was coming from a man who doesn't like musical theatre. By now we were just shaking our heads in disbelief, then David said it was 'faultless... and could be very big'.

MICHAEL: David vindicated our decision to go with 'Stars' because he pointed out that they do hear the same songs over and over again. After David, Alesha said it was one of the best auditions she'd ever seen.

TOM: All of these people are such huge names in the industry, so for them to give us such positive comments was incredibly reassuring. If we had any doubts about our band then they were gone.

RICHARD: Remember, I was worried we might be ridiculed, so the sense of relief was pretty massive.

MICHAEL: I will be honest with you, I was waving to my family, soaking in the applause and all these amazing compliments from the judges, so once they had given us their comments, I was about to walk off but then Alesha said, 'Right, we've got to vote,' and I thought, *Oh my God, I completely forgot about that.*

TOM: By this stage we knew we were going to get good votes, but it was still great to actually hear them all say yes.

JAMIE: I was already overwhelmed, so when Simon closed the comments by adding, 'You know what, Britain really has got talent, it's four yeses,' it was just the best moment. We gave each other a hug, Simon gave us a thumbs-up and a 'Well done,' then we all walked off.

MATT: The interview with Ant and Dec was shot as soon as we came off the stage. We were all in our own world, shocked, overwhelmed, thinking, *What has just happened?* Then you've got Ant and Dec, these really famous household names, standing right next to you saying, 'How do you feel then?' It was so bizarre.

RICHARD: I didn't know what to say to them, I was still stunned, just thinking, *This is just crazy. We've done it...*

JAMIE: By now I was just completely in bits, it was such an amazing experience. It just meant *so much*.

MICHAEL: Right after chatting to Ant and Dec, we had to go to a holding room where they videoed us walking downstairs. Then we had to go upstairs to be interviewed by Stephen Mulhern for the spin-off show, *Britain's Got More Talent*. He is really funny and had all these really cheeky and inappropriate questions for us.

RICHARD: The questions were really personal and, remember, we hadn't been together very long so when he was saying things like, 'Who has slept with the most women?' and 'Put yourself in a line in order of who is the best looking', it was really awkward. I just said, 'Put me last, I don't want to upset anyone!'

MICHAEL: It felt really strange because this audition was on 13th February and we had only met as a five-piece in mid-January. So we were essentially still getting to know one another. I was thinking, *I can't say I'm better looking than anyone else!* Fortunately the interview was never aired! As we were finally leaving, there were still a few people standing around in the entrance area and when we walked through I heard someone say, 'Oh my God there's that band!' That was really strange. A few of them came over and got selfies with us and you could see they were texting their mates and were quite excited. That was a really odd feeling. Nice, but a bit of a shock.

JAMIE: We were all so drained and overwhelmed. Tom, Matt and Rich wanted to get back to see their girlfriends, because it was Valentine's Day the next day. Michael and I wanted to have a quick drink, but we were so tired we weren't about to have a big night.

MATT: As we finally walked out of the auditions, I remember thinking, *What now?*

TOM: Hey, boys, do you remember what the woman asking for a selfie in the foyer said to us? She came over and said, 'Tonight we have seen the winners of *Britain's Got Talent*.'

CHAPTER 3

THE DELIBERATION ROUND

JAMIE: The first round of the *Britain's Got Talent* auditions was just so exciting. As I said, for me it was just incredibly overwhelming. It's only in the days after that you start to process what happened and that's when you realise that actually, even though we got four 'yeses', that didn't mean we were through to the semi-final. Next up is the so-called 'Deliberation Round'. That's when the four judges look at everyone they said 'yes' to – somewhere in the region of about 200 acts – and whittle the group down to about 45. If you are not in that 45 or so then that's it, game over.

Before the audition was actually aired on TV, we were all still very nervous. We were a boy band doing musical theatre – it was still something new and perhaps a risk. We felt quietly confident they would treat us well on screen, but you never know. I couldn't stop thinking about it. At this point we were not allowed to tell anyone, but it was pretty much all I thought about, 24/7.

TOM: The week after the first audition was very weird. You go home, brush your teeth, go to bed, wake up, eat breakfast, and then you all go back to work. And for me that was back at the Japanese restaurant. The guys at work knew I sang because I would often be singing to myself while tidying up after the final customer had left. So on the one hand everything is exactly the same as before the audition. Except *nothing* is the same because it's all you can think about, all the time. Potentially your whole future is in the balance.

MATT: I just kept thinking, *What do we do now?* It is all you want to talk about to anybody but you know you are not supposed to.

RICHARD: So now there was this wait to see whether or not we were through the Deliberation Round. Meanwhile, I went back to busking and labouring – back to my normal life.

JAMIE: We were told we would be shown on the first episode of *Britain's Got Talent* that year. When the day finally arrived, we all watched it at home with our families and friends. When we got the standing ovation from the audience and the judges, everyone around me cried. I am not kidding, my phone *exploded*, we had 9,000 new followers on Twitter within five minutes, then my friend Jade from Little Mix tweeted about us and we got even more people following us. It was crazy.

RICHARD: It was fascinating to watch the audition and I was *so* relieved that we came across well. Just after we'd finished singing, Ant said, 'Wow! What an audition!' Then after we'd walked off, the comments kept coming. Amanda said, 'I felt so overwhelmed with how good they were, oh my God.'

MATT: The one thing that we obviously didn't see at the time – because we had gone off stage – was Simon's last comment, which was 'That's a hit record.'

JAMIE: When Simon said that, we all sent about a million text messages out, 'Did you hear what Simon just said?' Instantly my phone went mad!

MICHAEL: Mine too! I couldn't actually get mine to work properly because it was just swamped with messages and tweets.

RICHARD: I stood up in my living room, punched the air and shouted, 'Yes!'

TOM: That was a shock, to have the head of this huge global company say that was incredible.

MATT: We noticed that they were playing Susan Boyle's version of 'I Dreamed A Dream', also from Les Misérables, in the background. That's obviously a very emotional song and brilliantly performed. It set the mood, it aligned us with successful musical theatre performers and it was a genius idea.

RICHARD: It was also fun to watch it back because a few members of our families were backstage on the day and they got to be extras in the background. It makes me laugh but there's one clear shot of the back of my dad's head!

JAMIE: Away from Britain's Got Talent, Collabro still had work to do. Before we did the Hammersmith audition, we'd already been booked to go on a tour of Pontins holiday camps, so in between the first audition and the Deliberation Round, that's what we did.

MICHAEL: We rented a car for the tour but when we went to pick it up, the only one they had available was much smaller than the one we had booked. Poor Richard was in the back of the car; I don't think Tom and Matt were very happy because he's so broad.

RICHARD: Tell me about it! Jamie and Michael were driving and I was crammed in the back with Tom and Matt. It was quite funny – although probably not for them! We had a good laugh on the road though. We actually sang tons in the car and practised a lot of our harmonising. It was the first time I really saw the band properly working as a unit.

MATT: Pontins was a great idea for us because we spent a good deal of time together, we became really good friends, plus there were plenty of shows in front of decent crowds. Some nights it was a fairly sparse crowd but other nights were pretty big. I think the biggest audience we played in front of was around 2,000. We even did some signing sessions for holidaymakers who had seen the *Britain's Got Talent* audition. At each park we stayed in little chalets and after each show we would sit around on the end of beds and chairs, just talking for hours and getting to know each other better.

MICHAEL: I set up a room rota so that everyone got to share with everyone else. I can honestly say that we didn't argue once, genuinely. It was fun too – most of the parks had basketball courts, table tennis and loads of sports so we'd play all that together. A lot of them were by the seafront too, so we'd walk along there and chat about the show and what might be coming next. It was just really easy-going.

TOM: Pontins was the first time we had spent any extended period of time together. We came together for rehearsals for a few hours or a day across a week or so, but we were together on this trip for five days, 24 hours a day. For me, I always think when you get a group of people together in such close proximity for so long, it is inevitable that there will be conflict. Even if it is just two people, as soon as you get into a group there are always opinions and people will not see eye to eye. That is what I worry about. But we didn't fall out at all; everyone got on really well and got to know each other a lot better. I kept worrying that something was going to go wrong, someone was going to fall out, but it was the complete opposite.

JAMIE: One particular night we went back to the chalet and all had a drink and a laugh together for the first time. Then as the night wore on we just opened up to each other and talked about all sorts of stuff. We went around the circle and said what we liked about each other, we talked a little bit about our back stories, our families, friends and childhood. It was the first time I had seen the boys for who they really are. Their personalities came out. That was really nice.

RICHARD: We would do half an hour singing and then an hour signing photos and posters. People loved it, which was really weird but also fantastic to get that reaction. There were some classic moments on that trip. One time we were on stage performing and during a break between songs someone came up to us and said, 'It's my mum's 70th birthday, can you present this balloon to her please?' We were more than happy to oblige so we called this lady's name out and asked her to come up on stage. We thought it would be a nice, *brief* interlude but I looked over to where she was and immediately saw that she couldn't walk unaided. She was really shaky on her feet – bless her. Anyway, it seemed like it took her about an hour to walk to the stage with her son holding her arm. I was like, 'That's it, come on, keep going, come on...'

She eventually made it to the stage and we gave her this balloon and wished her happy birthday. That's when it dawned on me... *Now she has to walk all the way back!*

MICHAEL: Some of the Pontins parks provided a little dressing room for us and because it was around Easter time, they were often full of these bags of chocolate eggs, the sort you'd get from a pound shop. That was a really nice gesture because not all of the parks necessarily fed us and we lived off these little chocolate eggs for most of the week! I've got a really sweet tooth so that was fine by me.

TOM: We did seem to go down very well. One night a holidaymaker came up to us and – right in front of the Pontins staff – she said, 'You are too good for this place.' It was really embarrassing.

MICHAEL: Looking back I think we were gaining voters all the time during those Pontins dates. Obviously people might enjoy our performance on the night but also we signed a load of posters and flyers, and you never know how many people enjoy our show and then feel moved to vote. Plus they might go home and tell their friends about us. So it can network out pretty quickly. The whole week was a really good experience – I really enjoyed it.

THE DELIBERATION ROUND

JAMIE: After that tour of Pontins I felt really buoyant. I did think to myself, *We can go somewhere with this band, we can do this, people seem to be really liking us and maybe we have really got a shot at this.* We started to feel during that week that if we took Collabro to a bigger crowd they might like it even more.

We'd got the call to say that we were in the 45 acts to make it through to the Deliberation Round which was absolutely amazing news. Like I said before, this didn't mean we were through to the semi-final, though, just that we had made it through to the top 45 or so acts. For that show, you go in for a really long day's filming where eventually you are invited into a room with a few others acts and the judges break the news to you about whether you have made it through to the live semi-finals. Understandably the atmosphere backstage during the day is extremely tense.

RICHARD: When I heard we were into the Deliberation Round, I thought, *This is awesome!* but we were all very aware they could just be setting this up to knock us down.

TOM: We'd been in the first audition weeks before, so it felt like we had to wait ages and ages for the Deliberation Round. We didn't want to dare to assume we were through to the semi, just in case it didn't happen. They could have just decided since the audition that, actually, a musical theatre boy band wasn't the kind of act they were looking for this year, after all.

We arrived first thing with everyone else but we were in the very last group of acts to be seen and filmed, right at the end of the day. In between the two we didn't actually film much, it was mostly just sitting around waiting to find out our fate. So it was another massively long and nerve-wracking *Britain's Got Talent* day!

RICHARD: We had made quite good friends with one of the producers of the show by this point and when we saw him early on during the Deliberation day we asked him if we'd got through. He replied, 'I don't know that kind of information!' and I said, 'You totally do!' but he reassured us that he didn't and in the end we believed him.

MICHAEL: They gave us a meal ticket to the pub next door to where the show was being filmed and we sat in there and watched the rugby. It was England versus Wales in the Six Nations and the game helped distract us from all the nerves and waiting around. During the day, loads of people were coming to the pub having got through, so we were thinking, *Is there going to be any space left for us?* Then we saw another boy band called Jack Pack go through who a lot of people thought were our main competition.

MATT: I thought, *If this doesn't go well today, then we will have to go another route, because I really want this now, I want to go for this because we have something.* However, the more we waited the more nervous we got. We saw some acts that were brilliant but didn't get through. Then we saw other acts we weren't so sure about who did get through so we couldn't work out what was going on. The day sort of tricks you; it plays with your mind.

RICHARD: Matt's right, you try and judge it: 'maybe because we are last it's a good sign? Surely they wouldn't make us wait all day if they want to get rid of us... would they?'

JAMIE: Eventually we were called to go to the room where the judges would deliver their verdict. This was it. They showed us through,

THE DELIBERATION ROUND

X marked the spot on the stage floor, ready for our fate. We were in the middle of a trio of acts alongside Lucy Kay and Eva Iglesias, who both got standing ovations after their first auditions, so that was surely a good sign?

MATT: When we walked into the room everything was dead silent and we just stood there on the marks, waiting for the judges to arrive.

RICHARD: The building we were sent into for the judges' decision was gorgeous, like a magnificent town hall, with sweeping stairs and all these period features and pillars. I'm surprised I remember that sort of detail because I mostly remember being absolutely petrified. Then the judges walked in – the waxworks again – still looking amazing, still very surreal.

TOM: Alesha did a speech about how this year's competition had been the highest standard ever, that obviously there wasn't a place for everyone, that they had to cut it down somehow, and that it had been really tricky for the judges, etc. – all this stuff. We were just standing there totally on edge. It was so nerve-wracking, even for someone as laid-back as me!

MATT: Then she said, 'Anyway, I have made a decision and I won't keep you waiting any longer'... but then she proceeded to wait for about five minutes! They had some camera work to do or something, but it was just so ironic that she said that and then did the exact opposite. It was hilarious, actually, because at one point Simon put his hands on his head and said, 'Oh come on!'

RICHARD: Lucy was standing next to me crying and I wanted to hug her but it was all I could do to stop my heart beating out of my chest, I was so anxious.

MATT: As soon as Alesha said she wouldn't keep us waiting any longer, all I could hear in the room was breathing.

TOM: Eventually she broke her silence but even then it was with a twist. She said, 'I'm sorry to have to tell you...' and when she said that my heart absolutely sank.

JAMIE: *Oh no...*

... 'You are through to the semi-finals!'

JAMIE: We just went completely crazy! It was the best feeling.

RICHARD: I did this massive rugby yell at the top of my voice. I was so happy, I didn't know who to hug first, I was hugging everyone. This was such a big deal.

MATT: We all cried once we found out, it was very emotional. All the lads hugged each other and I ran straight across and gave Eva and Lucy a hug too. That was such a nerve-wracking day.

JAMIE: That moment when Alesha paused was just horrendous. Then we all exploded. There are such extremes of emotion throughout the whole process. It is the most intense experience.

We had done it. We were through to the live semi-finals of *Britain's Got Talent*. The whole crazy journey wasn't over yet.

CHAPTER 4

THE *BRITAIN'S GOT TALENT* SEMI-FINAL

TOM: Once again, after we'd filmed the Deliberation Round it was straight back to normality. When you are doing a show like *Britain's Got Talent*, there's this really odd contrast between normal life and the TV shows. It's such a strange time – exciting but strange.

MATT: Someone asked me the other day when we felt like we could win, was it in the lead up to semi-finals maybe? To be perfectly honest we never thought, *We are going to win this*. We were more pragmatic; we thought, *Let's get through this round, see who else is left in the competition, start again, rehearse all week, get ready for the next stage.*

JAMIE: So here we are then, Matt. The next stage. The semi-final of *Britain's Got Talent* is a big deal. My mum was sceptical, though, as we headed towards the semi-final performance. She knows how quickly these things can change and she'd seen me try so hard for so many years, so I guess she was just worried for me. We were all really excited and growing in confidence. It helped that we were on the very first semi-final, so we could just crack on. As it turned out, we stormed through to the final.

TOM: We ran through a number of song options in preparation for the performance. Some of the ideas fell flat and maybe didn't have the same vibe as 'Stars' did; they just didn't give us the same feeling.

JAMIE: We all felt 'Bring Him Home' was a really good song for us to do. *Les Misérables* meant so much to all of us, so there was never any doubt that we would connect with that song.

MATT: However, due to the semi-final being live and run with military precision, we had to be specific with the length of the song. So our choice – 'Bring Him Home' – had to be cut down. We rehearsed and rehearsed and rehearsed this shorter version and eventually it started to feel natural.

JAMIE: It is just a fantastic song. There were some doubts, partly because we didn't want people to think we were just a *Les Misérables* tribute act. We tried 'Who Wants To Live Forever', which we knew from the Queen musical, and quite a few other songs too. Then we rehearsed 'Bring Him Home' in a room with some of the *Britain's Got Talent* crew in rehearsals and a few of the producers cried. We knew then: this was the song.

TOM: I remember that happening. They said that was our best song choice and that it gave them the same vibe as 'Stars' had done at the first audition.

MICHAEL: We were so busy rehearsing and working through the song choices that we didn't have much time to be anxious. From the very start of the whole *Britain's Got Talent* process, I said to myself, I am not going to have any preconceptions or any huge hopes until we have performed on that stage at the semi-final and I stuck to that. I hadn't taken any time off from the petrol station – so I was literally working there one day then the next day I was in rehearsals for *Britain's Got Talent* then back at the petrol station again. A few people approached me at the petrol station to chat about the band, but that might have had something to do with the 'Vote Collabro' posters in the window!

TOM: I completely agree with you, Michael. We felt better in ourselves for the semi. Without sounding too cocky, I felt reasonably confident by now. There are always nerves and you never really know how it is going to go, but I kept reminding myself of how well it went last time. Plus we actually knew 'Bring Him Home' even better than 'Stars', so I didn't feel any particular nerves about getting the song itself wrong – it was more anxiety about the performance as a whole, how we might be received and how it could look on TV.

MATT: The semi-final was in Fountain Studios in Wembley. It is a smaller venue and more intimate than Hammersmith, so both the audience and the judges feel closer. It is actually much smaller than you think it will be.

MICHAEL: The problem with being aired on the first semi-final is that people might forget about you by the end of the week. That was a concern.

RICHARD: As mentioned, there were loads of rehearsals and a soundcheck the day before; then the day itself was completely nuts.

JAMIE: I think semi-final day was all right, actually. You do a rehearsal of the whole show so you know who you are up against. Just like on the previous days, everyone arrived early and was sitting there from 8am till late at night after the live show. In between times we rehearsed in the morning, then got hair and make-up done, then they touched that up all day – it was endless. I wasn't too nervous this time because I felt that we were good and I knew that we had rehearsed like crazy.

MATT: Every element of *Britain's Got Talent* is rehearsed over and over again. So, for example, all the semi-final acts had to rehearse the moment when Ant and Dec tell them who is through to the next round. We all did run-throughs of the countdown and each time they'd 'eliminate' a certain act so that we all knew where to walk off if we didn't get through.

MICHAEL: When they rehearsed the results show, they would choose different acts each time to 'go through' but they never called us, so we always practised leaving the stage as if we'd been eliminated from the show. We weren't sure what to make of that. Was that a bad sign? Rehearsing leaving the show even before you have sung live on TV is a bit intense!

TOM: The rehearsal order doesn't have any meaning at all – it is just completely random. They just have to run with whatever gets the best rehearsal work done at the time. They have simply got to make sure that the show runs smoothly.

MATT: Another massive change behind the scenes which very few people would have noticed was that we had to use what are called 'in-ears', which are tiny monitors – not unlike a hearing aid in size and shape – that fit into your ear and allow you to hear the music and your band-mates over the noise of the crowd.

TOM: This was the very first time in any of our performing careers that we'd had to use in-ears. It was strange at first because as a group we are accustomed to being physically close and able to hear one another sing, but as soon as you put the in-ears in place, it is a completely different sound. It is hard to tell exactly what the audience are hearing, compared to what you can hear in your in-ears. You might feel that technically you are getting it right but you haven't actually got a clue how it sounds out there for the crowd. We had two days to rehearse with the in-ears. It was almost like learning to sing as a group all over again. Sometimes if the voices are far too loud in the in-ears, you completely lose the track so you don't know where you are; you can count it in your head but that's not always completely in time. However, if the track is far too loud, you can't hear yourself or the other singers. You occasionally see a group on TV and think, *They weren't quite together*. It is not always because they can't perform well, it might be because the mix is wrong in their ears and they can't actually hear what they are doing. It is a real challenge when you are not used to in-ears.

RICHARD: Early in the day one of the main producers came into the holding room where all the acts were and said, 'Right, out of the tens of thousands of acts who auditioned for *Britain's Got Talent* this year, you are all in the semi-final!'

That was really exciting, but building up to the performance on the actual semi-final day was really difficult, because it is so long-winded. We did more filming and interviews; we bumped into people; we met all these other acts and all the time trying to find out the running order for the night's show and to figure out if it made a difference or not. I've got to be honest, that day is such a blur to me, it's all merged into one.

JAMIE: I was backstage and wanted to know everything: the running order, who was feeling nervous, who was relaxed and if there were any clues from the production team as to the voting. I am really nosy, so out of all the band you can guarantee that I will know the names of everybody in a room, where they were last night and if they are happy or not. I know all the inside goss on everyone. I really like being 'in the know'.

MICHAEL: Eventually they settled on a running order with us going on last. We were really pleased with that because it is always seen as the best slot.

RICHARD: As we were last to come on, we obviously got to hear all these other acts get their comments first, and it might've just been my nerves but Simon Cowell seemed really grumpy, he didn't seem in a very good mood. All the time I was thinking, *I've got to get this performance right tonight more than any other performance in my life,* yet you're also dealing with all this new stuff that is completely out of your comfort zone – people dressing you, styling you, applying make-up and using the in-ears. It can be very hard to focus on the song.

MATT: Absolutely. If a producer says anything to you that sticks in your mind, any little thing, you read something into that. They might come up to you at the end of the soundcheck and say, 'Great performance,' so you'd think that was a good sign. Or maybe they were just being polite? Funnily enough, I bumped into Simon Cowell on the stairs during semi-final day and he shook my hand and said how well we were doing. Straight away I ran back to the lads and told them. However, the bottom line is, the results are down to the public vote.

MICHAEL: Backstage there was this little monitor screen that I liked to keep an eye on, which showed what was being broadcast on TV. I felt more informed that way. Some of the boys didn't like to watch it, but I just felt that if we didn't get through, then I might as well have watched the show!

RICHARD: In the last few seconds before we were called onstage for our performance, I was really hyped up. Now we were singing live to millions of people so if we screwed up, there was no second take; this was the real deal. I get very pumped before a performance, so I was giving a team talk to the boys, slapping them across the back, and telling them to do this for their families. The rugby player was coming out in me, I guess! When you play rugby you really are an integral part of a team and I think that is where a lot of my actions come from when I am with the boys. I am very team oriented. I bring rugby to what we are doing because that is all I have ever really known. Hey, hang on, that must be the first time that rugby has been brought to musical theatre!

TOM: Probably, Richard, yes! Before every gig we also put our hands in a circle and say, 'Collabro!' Then we feel together as a group. It is really nice.

MATT: Standing at the side of stage, I said, 'Lads, this needs to be the performance of our lives!' and after Richard's famous team talk we were all ready.

RICHARD: I think I scared a few of them with my pep talk this time. It is an ongoing joke that the boys are more scared of my team talks than they are of the actual performance.

MATT: 'Bring Him Home' was the first song we ever performed together, it was from a musical that meant a lot to all of us, we had rehearsed intensely and knew every single note and detail of the performance. All we had to do now was go out there and deliver. On the night, when TV viewers saw the band name 'Collabro' written in blue neon across their whole screen at home, we were being hustled out on to the stage to take our places and then suddenly, BANG!, we were on stage and the music was starting.

MICHAEL: I was caught out by exactly that! It was so fast from being at the side of stage to starting to sing. We each had these square blocks to stand on and every time we had rehearsed it we'd walked behind the blocks and stepped up onto them. Anyway, on the night because some stage crew were adjusting microphones, we had to walk in front of the blocks and it's amazing how something like that can sometimes put you on edge. Then I spotted this sea of red 'Vote Collabro' T-shirts (that I'd had printed for our families) in the audience, which was very reassuring. I was busy waving at my sister and thinking, *Amanda looks amazing*, then suddenly the music started!

JAMIE: I loved the stage set-up for our semi-final performance. The lighting was very cool too. It felt good, it felt polished, we were ready; I really enjoyed that performance. This time Richard's first line was much more relaxed, or at least it sounded that way.

RICHARD: Thanks, Jamie. Having to use in-ears was very hard though. You do get used to it but it wasn't my preferred way of singing. I had been having trouble with that first note of 'Bring Him Home' in rehearsals. If you listen carefully, I don't exactly crack on the word 'hear' but I do sing something different, something I had never done before and had never even practised, just a little click at the end of the note. Fortunately it seemed to go down really well. We were just performing for our careers – we simply gave it everything.

MICHAEL: Richard was understandably nervous; he has never breathed in that first line like that before.

MATT: I was thinking: Please do well, Richard, please do well, but actually I had the utmost faith in him. I knew he would deliver and, of course, he did, so the song was off to a great start.

JAMIE: As the performance started, that's when it dawned on me that we were singing live in front of 12 million people. I tried really hard to think about something else, to focus on just the people in the audience, the immediate auditorium. It is very hard to visualise 12 million people watching you. Plus it was live and anything could go wrong so we just relied on each other to get through it. We all just went for it. We knew this was it.

MATT: 'Bring Him Home' is different to 'Stars' because the former is softer, more emotional; it is a slower build-up so people tend to sit back and listen, they don't get taken away by the song as quickly. We had the in-ears so we couldn't hear much feedback from the crowd anyway, but I sensed it was going well.

MICHAEL: Then it was Tom and me. I remember practising so much with Tom to get our timing perfect so that we were singing in absolute unison.

TOM: Before the performance, we went through this song in minute detail. For example, the line where we sing 'in my need' was pored over so many times so that Michael and I knew exactly how to get the clean end to the sound that we wanted, with just a touch of vibrato, but at the same time not clashing with each other. That was really precise. There are so many little elements and details that a lot of people don't think about. We like to be meticulous.

MATT: This time there was a key difference in our approach to the performance, because as a band you have to play to the camera – in other words, to the millions of people watching. If you just sing to the four judges and the people at home can only see you looking down at the floor, it's not going to work. In a weird way you have to ignore everything going on in the studio and just play to the camera, look down the lens, flirt with the camera and just hope that you connect with the people at home. So that was an important shift. We were singing to the entire country now.

MICHAEL: The in-ears were challenging and it was pretty dark in there so we couldn't really see how the audience was reacting. The boys sounded really good in my in-ears, so I just went with it and really enjoyed the performance. I really don't want this to sound arrogant but when we got on the stage I knew we were going to sing well; we had rehearsed so much and we were ready so I wasn't worried about that. Plus I didn't have a solo so I didn't have to worry too much. It was more about whether people at home voted for us. Your vote of confidence in yourself can only take you so far.

MATT: When we hit the big build-up around the lyrics 'the summers die', it felt like a big moment. I could feel the momentum increasing.

JAMIE: Then I had to sing 'And I am old and will be gone, God', and it felt good. I felt like we were really nailing the performance. I was so proud of us all.

TOM: I am the highest voice out of the group and one particularly nerve-wracking moment for me came when I was blasting out 'If I die...' It is a really high note but it also needs some power and I was just hoping I could get the combination right under such intense pressure. Fortunately it seemed to go okay.

RICHARD: I have the last note as well and I had to hold that note for quite a long time, which was not easy. I think you can actually see my face stretching around my mouth to hold the note. I don't want to sound inappropriate but it looks like I've had a mini stroke, my mouth is going sideways because I'm desperate to try and hold on to this note.

JAMIE: Once again we were delighted to see the audience and the judges' reaction – both of which were great. We knew we had done well: we'd got another standing ovation – that was two out of two!

MATT: In the world of musical theatre, getting a standing ovation is a massive achievement. The fact that it had now happened to us again was just unreal.

MICHAEL: Simon wasn't the last one to stand up this time, which was incredible. Even the friends and family of other acts were clapping and standing up which was really nice considering we were in direct competition. Then they asked me to speak and I just tried to articulate how much we wanted to succeed and how hard we had tried.

MATT: We then stepped forward and waited for the judges' comments. Even though it is up to the public vote, the judges' comments can influence that vote very heavily. We hoped they would be good, but – at the risk of repeating ourselves! – you never know. Thankfully they were really good comments again. Now it was up to the viewing public; it was out of our hands. We'd done everything we could.

MICHAEL: Since we were the last ones to perform on the night, we then had to go through a number of interviews, so some of us didn't even get a chance to vote for ourselves! I was thinking, *Hang on, that's a vote lost!*

RICHARD: I managed to cram a few votes in. We came off stage and I was straight onto my phone voting away; I was texting people, getting on Facebook – it was so hectic. We only had about half an hour till the results show, so I had no time to lose!

TOM: It was actually quite refreshing by the time of the semi-final, because for the first time we didn't know any secrets that the audience wasn't aware of. They had caught up with the show in real time. It is a bit stressful when you're not allowed to tell people anything!

MATT: We were waiting backstage for the results show to roll around and we felt quite good; we felt we had done our best and that the performance had gone well. At one point, on that little screen backstage, they broadcast a recap of all the night's performances, along with the phone numbers to vote for. When our little snippet came up it sounded and looked good. We swapped a few glances and nods; I think we knew then that we'd done well.

MICHAEL: You want to have faith in yourself; you want to remember the standing ovation, to know that we all hit our harmonies and that we have faith in the arrangement and our endless rehearsals. But the unpredictability of *Britain's Got Talent* is what makes it so entertaining. You end up thinking, Maybe the public found it more entertaining seeing a man in a pink Lycra suit singing 'It's Raining Men'? You just don't know.

JAMIE: In the semi-final we felt Jack Pack and Bars And Melody were the biggest threats to us getting through, at least in terms of other boy bands. We actually thought Lucy Kay hadn't been played up that much, but we knew she was fantastic. When she sang in the semi-final she was just outstanding, so we thought she was now the one to beat. It was so nerve-wracking again.

MICHAEL: Luckily, waiting for the results flew by: the crew was doing more hair and make-up; we were getting ready and being interviewed. Then suddenly it was time to stand on stage for the results show. As they started to read out who was going home, I suddenly panicked and thought, *Oh my God, we might be leaving the show right now.*

MATT: That was the most terrifying moment in the semi-final, waiting for them to say who had won the public vote and was going straight through. So when they said it was Collabro, we just went nuts again!

JAMIE: That was another big Collabro moment. That was it; we were in the final of *Britain's Got Talent*. It was massive.

MICHAEL: Straight away we had to leave the stage and be interviewed by Ant and Dec. I remember looking at my phone after the semi-final and I had more than 120 text messages and that's not even counting WhatsApp, Facebook or Twitter.

RICHARD: I think we jumped 10,000 followers on Twitter from that one performance.

JAMIE: We later found out that we won almost 63 per cent of the votes, so we absolutely knocked it out of the ballpark. Darcy Oake came second with 15.5 per cent. That was a big win for us. I think it was the biggest winning percentage of votes for the whole series. We are very proud of that. It shows we must have had some kind of audience.

RICHARD: Then we had to wait for absolutely ages to be filmed for the end of *Britain's Got More Talent*. Louie Spence was there and he was doing this dance for Darcy Oake, it was hilarious. Stephen Mulhern asked us to describe the way we were feeling through an animal expression and I just remember mooing... on live TV. Yes, mooing.

MATT: We spent a little while with our families in the holding area of the café with some champagne. Obviously we were absolutely shattered by this point so we just had a couple of drinks with them then eventually all went home.

The whole time though, we kept saying to each other, 'We are through to the Final of *Britain's Got Talent!* How has that happened?'

It felt so incredible.

CHAPTER 5

THE *BRITAIN'S GOT TALENT* FINAL

MICHAEL: After our semi-final, we all watched every other semi to see who our competition was going to be. I watched some of the semi-finals with my family. During that week I also worked two or three days at the petrol station.

JAMIE: A big upside of being in the very first semi-final was that we had almost two weeks to rehearse before the actual final itself. In the semi we'd all been reasonably relaxed – to a point – but we were all pretty nervous about the final. The stakes were just *so* high. I had to go out for a couple of drinks in the middle of the second week because I was so tense; I just needed to unwind a little bit otherwise it would've affected my performance. I think by that point in the process there is a degree of tiredness that sets in. I was fatigued and pretty much running on empty. You just keep going. Adrenalin is an amazing thing. So is determination.

TOM: I took that whole week off right before the show. That was nice although it was worrisome because I didn't know where my next month's rent was coming from. As exciting as appearing on that show is, the reality for me was that if we did fail then I would be back at home and unable to pay my rent.

MICHAEL: All that week we were trying to decide which song to perform in the final. We rehearsed various options, memorised the arrangements, worked with a vocal coach, and even went to meet the orchestra that was going to be playing with us – no cheesy karaoke backing track this time!

MATT: There was no complacency from us after the semi; it was just straight back into rehearsals. We all felt we really needed to step up our game. In fact, we wanted to do something completely different. So we came up with the idea of performing 'Somewhere Over The Rainbow'. Like Jamie said earlier, the one thing we didn't want was to come across as a *Les Misérables* tribute band.

MICHAEL: I would add to that that we also knew that Jack Pack and Lucy were doing a different song. We didn't just want to sound like we were repeating ourselves.

MATT: Then we heard that Simon Cowell really wanted us to do 'Stars' again. We were told that he felt quite strongly about that. That was a difficult moment because to us, at that point, to sing 'Stars' again seemed like we risked people accusing us of being one-dimensional.

TOM: In some interviews it had almost become a little joke about being a *Les Misérables* tribute act. We'd say, 'We do have other songs in our repertoire, you know!'

JAMIE: We were also struggling to cut our version of 'Somewhere Over The Rainbow' down enough to make it sound like a complete, coherent song in just two minutes.

MICHAEL: Simon Cowell is very intimately involved with his shows backstage. He doesn't just turn up and pretend to know people or have nothing to do with the songs they are going to perform. He thinks about each act, he talks to them about his ideas, he will often let them run with their thoughts but if he feels strongly about something he will say so. For example, he had long chats with Lucy about her song choice and they discussed at length about performing 'Nessun Dorma'. He gets incredibly involved. Obviously with someone as high profile as that, if you are going against his judgement then you have to be pretty confident you are making the right decision. So we were very flattered that he was so keen for us to do 'Stars', because it meant he wanted us to put on a good show. He'd said, 'People love "Stars", it is a showstopper.'

RICHARD: One day during that final week I'd been out busking in George Street in Brighton, essentially to try to drum up some votes and support locally. I earned a little bit of money then went to the KFC and sat down to eat my lunch. My mobile rang and it was Jamie. He is the organiser of the band so I assumed it would be about timings of rehearsals or something like that.

JAMIE: Richard's not lying. I have always been very sensible. I plan. All the boys get sick of it! I plan ten steps ahead all the time. In my head I always have this massive spider's web of plans; I love doing that. It's just the way I am.

RICHARD: Anyway, on this occasion he didn't want to talk about organising something, he just said, 'Simon Cowell doesn't want us to do "Somewhere Over The Rainbow".' I asked him what the alternative was and when he said, 'Stars' again, I was really frustrated. I just didn't agree with the idea. We were much more than just a two-song, one musical band. Jamie was really good though because he listened to me and then he said, 'To be honest, Richard, I actually agree with Simon. I see what he is saying, this is a big moment and 'Stars' is a big song. I think it is a really good idea.' Eventually, I came around to the idea and I will be the first to admit that on the night it sounded great. I still think we would have done a fantastic job of 'Somewhere Over The Rainbow' and I still think we maybe could have won singing that song. But it is hard to argue with the boss!

TOM: To be fair, we know now that it couldn't have gone any better and it was completely the right choice.

MATT: So we went with the decision to do 'Stars' after all. However, we thought, *Okay, in that case let's step it up and do the song differently – let's put a key change in there.*

RICHARD: I will be honest here and say I wasn't massively into the key change idea either! I was worried it was too cheesy. Initially I felt quite strongly about that.

MICHAEL: The key change was hard because we were already singing that song pretty high. We could've dropped the entire key at the start and given ourselves an easier ride but we decided not to and instead went higher and bigger and better. It was actually only the day before the final that we were 100 per cent set on 'Stars'.

MATT: There was a lot of filming throughout that week of the final, as well as constant rehearsing, rehearsing, rehearsing. After the semi-final I'd finally handed my notice in at the kitchen showroom and we were all free to just rehearse. There's so much to practise: you run through your stage positioning, when you are going to look into camera, where you are going to stand and how the lighting will work. The one thing I'd always dreamt of as a performer was having a river of dry ice on stage as I sang... and for the final we got exactly that!

MICHAEL: Now, when I watch *The X Factor* or any reality talent show, I can completely sympathise with contestants because I know how many hours they have been rehearsing, recording, filming and waiting around. Perhaps inevitably I now look at those shows from another perspective.

Before Collabro I was a big fan of these shows. Now, I'm a huge fan. I admire the fact they offer opportunities to people who might otherwise struggle. One thing I find odd is when people say, 'I don't like those shows.' Why? Why do you need to put someone else down to make yourself feel better? I have always said to anyone trying to break into the entertainment industry to just go for it, give it a go. If you want something that badly, just ignore people who say things like that.

JAMIE: There was tons of press and interviews to do all that week, it's not just rehearsing and relaxing! There was lots of work too – it was such a hectic week. So the day before the final, for example, we did *Good Morning Britain* with Richard Arnold; we then had some phone interviews and a few more rehearsals, including the results show standing on the stairs. It was crazily busy!

MICHAEL: One Direction were performing at Wembley that week and when me, Matt and Jamie were getting the Tube home one night, loads of 1D fans were stopping us for pictures, shouting, 'Good luck for tomorrow!' It was the most amazing feeling. They were so nice to us.

MATT: We all had an early night before the final. We were up early in the morning and I remember opening my eyes and the light was shining through the hotel room curtains and my first thought was, *Today is the day, this is it: the biggest performance of our lives.* I went down and had some breakfast, then headed to the studio.

JAMIE: I didn't sleep the night before at all. How could I? Everything was riding on this performance.

MICHAEL: I couldn't sleep either. I wasn't feeling great when I got up. I remember sitting up in bed and thinking, *In 15 hours we will know who has won this...*

TOM: On the morning of the final, I was actually packing up to move house. Several weeks earlier, I'd handed in notice on my rented flat and coincidentally it just so happened that the moving date was the day after the *Britain's Got Talent* final. So on the morning of that last show I had to get my entire life packed and into boxes! Luckily all of my family was down for the show so that was a bonus because they were helping me move. Actually, I think that kind of helped my nerves, because there was so much to organise, to pack, to get sorted, I barely had a chance to get nervous.

JAMIE: Every single day – it doesn't matter what we're doing or where we are – when all the boys meet up we give each other a hug and say hello; that is how close we are as a group. That's exactly what we did when we arrived at the studios. We then sat down at the table in the holding room with the other acts, with whom we had become really good friends. I am all for competing against people, but actually everyone was so nice it was hard to see them as rivals. Then it was into hair and make-up really early with tons of filming throughout the day and yet more interviews – it was hectic.

TOM: We had so much respect for all the acts. When you are in *Britain's Got Talent* – and I suspect the other shows like *The X Factor* are much the same – you are in this kind of bubble for weeks. It's all very intense and you do become really good friends with people that you know are actually fighting against you.

MICHAEL: When we went on stage for our tech run Simon showed up and after our performance he clapped us and nodded to the producers. That felt good.

MATT: We decided to go with slightly more formal styling this time. Yes, we had made this stance about being a boy band in casual clothes that sang musical theatre, but we felt for the actual final it needed just a little step up in appearance. We weren't about to come on stage in really formal dinner jackets or trussed up in ties, but we did have jackets and shirts. We wanted to keep it young and fresh but at the same time there was a level of smartness that we felt was needed, which was hard to gauge. For the final we wore exactly what we wanted and I think we looked all right.

JAMIE: We had set our stall out at the very first audition – that was the moment when the country first saw Collabro, just these young lads singing musical theatre in the clothes they wore every day. That was the big statement and that was our trademark look. We felt that for the final we could deviate slightly from that, out of respect for the occasion as much as anything, without diluting our stance at all. It is about having that transformation.

TOM: As you know we've always said we are not the kind of people for suits, but as Jamie just said, when you are competing for a spot on the Royal Variety Performance you do want to look smarter. You can do that without a suit and tie.

MICHAEL: I had to change my shirt because the one they'd suggested had a closed collar with a tiepin and I felt like I was being choked. Too formal! I changed that for an open shirt.

MATT: By now I was really nervous. The final; 13 million people; yikes.

MICHAEL: Everyone was in costume, made up, rehearsed and ready by 3pm but the show didn't go live until 7:30pm. That is a long wait – let me tell you.

TOM: In rehearsals we did mock countdowns of the elimination, which was really bizarre. They even had to interview the 'winners', asking how it felt to win the competition. It was really surreal because we all acted out the final before it had even happened. It seems strange but the reality is that *Britain's Got Talent* is so time-sensitive, so precise, it is totally live and they have to have every single second of that show worked out perfectly. The amount of work that goes into each live show is just ridiculous.

JAMIE: Unfortunately I was having a lot of vocal trouble on the day of the final. My voice wasn't at its absolute best. I think it was maybe nerves. I never usually suffer like that but it was such intense pressure, so I had lost all of my top range. We had to switch a few parts around which was obviously unsettling but the boys were all so focused. We just worked it out, ran through it over and over again and nailed it.

MICHAEL: Jamie could barely talk; he was really struggling so we were worried about that. He just got on with it though like a real professional.

JAMIE: We were all fighting for it. I still felt nervous but as a group we had a real determination; we knew what we wanted, we were rehearsed and we were ready. I drew a lot of strength from the boys around me and I really felt we could deliver a great performance, even under such extreme pressure.

MICHAEL: Throughout the day the running order kept changing; we were seventh then we were eighth then we were fifth. When we found out we were the penultimate act before Lucy, we were really pleased. They normally do 'save the best till last' because it ends the show on a good note.

TOM: The nerves were definitely kicking in by the time the evening came round. Nerves are one of the worst things you can suffer from if you have IBS, so for a lot of the final day, I was sitting down in pain with quite a nasty stomach ache, just trying not to think about what was happening later.

MATT: Little Mix were performing that night and as they came off-stage they walked past us and wished us good luck (Ella Henderson had done the same in the semi-final). Cheryl Cole was backstage and she said, 'Good luck in the Final,' as well which was a massive boost.

RICHARD: There were lots of different celebrities just walking around. I saw Cheryl casually walking past – that's weird! – as well as Sunita and David Walliams. He came backstage a few times and he was really nice and very genuine.

MATT: Everyone who performed before us sounded and looked so good.

JAMIE: Paddy and Nico were brilliant. Jack Pack laid down their gauntlet, as did Bars And Melody. Darcy and John Clegg both did really well on the night. There were some really big players who had really made their mark. Lucy was coming after us and she had been so phenomenal in the semi, so we suspected that she'd also be one to beat. We just had to do an amazing job.

MICHAEL: Can you imagine watching nine other acts go before you and from about the fifth act, the judges were saying, 'You are amazing, you could win this!' We had seen the betting odds so we thought we might be in the top five with Bars And Melody as the winners. Jack Pack, Darcy Oake and Lucy were all up there too.

TOM: According to the bookies, Collabro and Bars And Melody were favourites to win. I just tried to keep away from that sort of thinking. We never presumed, we never thought, *We have won this.* We couldn't be so arrogant. It was always, *We will do our best in the hope that we will win.*

MICHAEL: I can honestly say, hand on heart, that I wasn't worried about winning. To me it didn't matter if someone else won, I just thought, *We will come where we come and we will stay together and do as much as we can with this band.*

RICHARD: Initially I wasn't thinking about Lucy at all and I don't mean that in any disrespectful way, of course. I remember watching Darcy Oake and thinking, *He is really good.* Even at this stage, we didn't think we were going to win; we thought we'd finish maybe third or maybe fourth. We knew we had a good fan base behind us so the likelihood was we were going to get decent votes but we didn't think we were going to win it. Sometimes I would say to the boys, 'We could win this,' but I never necessarily believed it myself, to be honest.

MATT: Finally, we got the call to start getting ready, so it was back into more hair and make-up; we checked our clothes, then lined up at the side of the stage, facing the auditorium. We put our in-ears in place and then we were all set. We had our usual team talk and I said, 'Sing like it is the last time you are ever going to sing, go for it, take every bit of emotion and use that, tell the story, this is the big one.' I don't mind admitting that by this point it was pretty terrifying. It was a big deal.

JAMIE: Our families were in the audience again with the red 'Vote Collabro' T-shirts and we could see them from the wings. Then we heard Ant and Dec introducing us… this was it: the most important performance of our career.

RICHARD: No standing on boxes this time. I had a little goatee beard as well! I was nervous for the opening line but I felt okay, it seemed to go well.

MATT: We'd had the conversation about needing to play to the camera, flirt with the public at home again. I was very conscious of that when my first lines came in after Richard's start.

JAMIE: I felt good when I came in; I was obviously wary of my voice but I had such faith in this group, such a belief that we had worked hard and that we could deliver. I think in this performance you can really see each of us living the part; we are acting the lyrics out like Matt said, not just singing a series of notes. I was just trying to inject as much emotion into my performance as possible.

TOM: Do you remember I mentioned my IBS giving me bad stomach ache throughout the day? Well, the amazing thing is that as soon as I get on stage, for any performance, not just the final of *Britain's Got Talent*, all of that pain goes away. It is the lead up to a performance that kills me, the anticipation, but the moment I step on stage, the nerves dissipate and I am absolutely fine.

MICHAEL: I was really grateful that I'd had a chance to sing as part of the group before my solo so I could check my in-ears were working. Mind you, if they hadn't been working I don't know exactly what I would have done!

TOM: At the start of the song I was a blank slate, just waiting for my moment to come in. Throughout the whole performance, I was thinking about the story behind the song and what it meant. I felt in the final we were a bit more animated – as a band we were a little more accustomed to the whole *Britain's Got Talent* environment. We felt more comfortable and I would like to think that shows in the performance.

MATT: When we all belted out, 'And so it must be, for so it is written,' it was a big moment. We were very determined – all five of us really fighting for our futures. Simon later said that is one of the aspects that he liked about us as a band, he said we had 'steel in our eyes' and knew what we wanted.

MICHAEL: It's true, at that moment we do look very determined. There was just so much riding on it.

JAMIE: Then the microphones came off their stands and we did our walk forward once again. I really felt like we were taking our performance to the audience and judges, I felt so proud. But I still had to focus; my concentration was so intense.

MATT: Another big moment was when Michael sang, 'Lord, let me find them' and you can hear everyone cheering.

MICHAEL: I was so nervous then – that was probably the worst I have ever sung that solo!

TOM: Then the big key change! After all the debate in the week leading up to the final, the key change felt amazing to do. As a consequence though, the lyrics 'I swear by the stars' were very high! I thought, *I'm not sure I can belt that note out because it is so high,* plus I wasn't too confident in my mix. But we pulled together for the big finale and nailed that performance.

JAMIE: We had done it and we all knew we'd performed as well as we could. I was so proud of us. As if the performance wasn't already an enormous moment in our lives, Simon Cowell was the first to give us a standing ovation.

TOM: That was unreal. *We have done it again,* I thought, *Every performance that we have done as a group up to this point, from Blackpool right through to the* Britain's Got Talent *final, we've had a standing ovation.*

TOM: It is great to think that we didn't do a performance on *Britain's Got Talent* where the judges didn't stand up. We should be really proud of that. The judges' comments were great too but you still never know what the public will decide. We had done the best we could do and we'd got an amazing reaction on every single show. By that point we were just praying and hoping...

RICHARD: We walked offstage and once again I was straight on my phone trying to vote!

JAMIE: That's funny really, because the winner tends to get something like two million votes.

RICHARD: Exactly! But you just do whatever you think will help. The voting window this time was about 15 minutes, but when I dialled our number it said, 'Sorry, the lines are now closed'. I was gutted!

JAMIE: It wasn't too bad: we'd performed very late in the running order so we didn't have too long to wait for the results show. I felt emotionally spent inside though, I was just trying to suppress any kind of emotion because it was so nerve-wracking. I have never been so scared in my life. Then Lucy Kay came on after us and was absolutely, totally brilliant!

MATT: We were all backstage and there was so much tension because after Lucy's song there was only one set of adverts and then it was back on air for the results. In what seemed no time at all, the call went out to go backstage and we were instructed to get into our positions to walk down the stairs for the results.

RICHARD: During the wait at the top of those stairs I was absolutely petrified. We all took our places and they started the countdown. For some reason, at this stage I was convinced we were going home. Convinced.

MATT: Ant and Dec started counting down, from eleventh place, then tenth, ninth... and we watched on as all these great acts had the dreaded red light fall on them as they were sent home, but still we weren't called out. That time on stage was terrifying; it was so anxious. Then suddenly the red light fell on Tom.

My heart sank; we were out. Disaster.

TOM: I felt this red light fall on me and then all the boys just looked at me... Are we out?

MICHAEL: It was actually shining over the Men In Heels but Tom was standing near enough to be caught in the red light! We didn't know that for a moment so I thought, *Oh my God, we are out.*

All the time I was standing there thinking, *Don't say us, don't say us, don't say us.* The biggest shock for me was when Paddy and Nico came ninth. I thought, *What?* She was the loveliest woman – she'd been teaching me little dance steps out the back. He was really nice as well, chatting to Jamie backstage in Spanish. I was really, really shocked when they were eliminated. I suddenly thought, *Gosh, we could come anywhere.*

MATT: They carried on calling out names until there were only four acts remaining: Bars And Melody, Lucy Kay, Jack Pack and us. Then they called out the act in fourth place and it was Jack Pack! We were totally stunned.

MICHAEL: We had a feeling the public would either vote for Jack Pack or us. So when they came fourth I thought, *At least we have won the battle of the boy bands,* although there never really was any battle because all those guys were so nice.

TOM: Then they said, 'The act in third place… will be revealed after the break…' They never tell any acts they are going to do that so we were like, 'Oh no!'

MATT: During that advert break I got everyone from the top three in a huddle and I said, 'Listen guys, this is it, it doesn't matter what happens now, none of us have lost, we have all won. We are all going to get something out of this, so no matter what happens, we have done it.'

MICHAEL: The Bars And Melody boys were great; they were telling us not to worry, even though they were only kids!

RICHARD: Then I said to the boys, 'Look, we have done the best we could, it is now in the hands of the voters, there is nothing more we can do. It has been an absolute ride. If it goes somewhere great, if it doesn't then we can still be so proud. Whatever happens next, I hope we can carry on this band and make sure we do that to the best of our ability.'

JAMIE: I wasn't sure what to think at that point. I did think there was a chance we could do it. After the reaction to the semi-final I thought, *Do you know what? We could actually win this. We could actually do something really big with this.* At the same time it almost seemed too much of a dream to dare to believe it.

TOM: Then they sent Bars And Melody home in third place.

RICHARD: I thought, *What? How is this happening?* They had been to America on huge TV shows; they had 200,000 followers on

Twitter. I was convinced they were going to win. So now it was down to Lucy and us...

MICHAEL: We really thought Bars And Melody would come top. That was a huge shock. I was so grateful people were voting for us and I was really shocked Bars And Melody were out. I think the fact that we were a five-piece dotted around the country helped with phone votes from all those locations. Maybe, I don't know.

MATT: Despite telling the boys a few moments before that we'd already achieved our goals, I suddenly wanted to win more than anything. When they said Bars And Melody had come third, it was a massive shock. There is a photo of us all at that exact moment and our jaws have just dropped to the floor. I couldn't believe it. We were in the top two. Then we had to move either side of Ant and Dec... for them to announce the winner.

JAMIE: We were so nervous. Crippled with nerves actually – it was completely overwhelming. On reflection, I think I was nervous because I was beginning to think we could actually win the competition.

MATT: The footage of Dec reading out the winner is really odd for me to watch because I don't remember any of it. Even watching it back, I have no recall whatsoever. I can only remember the one line.

Dec: *'Thousands auditioned, the lucky few made it to the semi-finals and tonight 11 acts gave the performance of their lives in a quite unforgettable final.'*

Ant: *'Now it all comes down to just two... one of you will leave here tonight with a quarter of a million pounds and a place on the bill at the Royal Variety Performance.'*

'The winner of Britain's Got Talent 2014 is...'

RICHARD: Once again it seemed like forever, just the longest pause, and I began to think, *We are not going to win, we are not going to win, we are not going to win.* I really thought I could feel those words coming... then right at the last moment I thought, *No, we have won this, we have got this!*

MICHAEL: I'd decided not to have any expression on my face when I was waiting for the winner to be announced. So I just put my head down.

JAMIE: I had my fists clenched and my arms straight down by my side – my nervous stance again.

TOM: That moment waiting was just endless. In those few seconds all these thoughts flash through your mind, *We have won, we haven't won, we have won, no, we haven't.*

MATT: It was horrible – even watching it back now makes the hairs on my neck stand up.

JAMIE: When Dec says, 'Collabro!' we just EXPLODED! We went nuts; you can see how much it means to us in the footage. If you look at my face at the exact moment Dec says 'Collabro', I am completely open-mouthed in shock. Then I just ran off to the back of the stage. I just couldn't believe it; I was in a state of total and utter shock.

MATT: I knocked out an invisible Mike Tyson, punching the air. Oh my God, we have won the whole thing, we have won *Britain's Got Talent*, we have won *Britain's Got Talent*... we have won *Britain's Got Talent!*

RICHARD: Boom! I fell to the floor, screaming and rolling around, and then I picked up Michael and bear-hugged him. I was screaming at the top of my lungs. I was quite literally hysterical with happiness.

MICHAEL: Richard just picked me up. I love watching that little clip over again. We just didn't know what to do. It was the most incredible feeling. I was so happy.

TOM: I saw Richard completely fall over; Jamie went to the back of the stage and didn't know what to do; I was just cheering and smiling – what a moment!

JAMIE: People often ask me how it felt when Dec read out our name as the winners. I honestly can't tell you, not in words. It's impossible to write down our feelings. It doesn't seem anywhere near enough to simply say it was brilliant – the most amazing feeling ever; a life-changing moment. I was so emotional, thinking about all those years of trying to break through. Now we'd won the biggest talent competition on TV.

MICHAEL: If you watch the clip and look at Jamie, he goes straight over to Lucy. What a star, even at that moment of total joy for himself, he went and gave her a hug.

JAMIE: I did, yes, because Lucy was so graceful. She wanted to win, she really wanted to win yet she was so pleased for us and so dignified. I went straight over and hugged her. She had been so lovely all the way through. What a phenomenal singer and an amazing woman.

MATT: They asked Jamie a question and given what he's just said, you can see why he was so emotional that he couldn't answer, so they turned to me. If they'd asked me a couple of seconds earlier I would have been the same, but I managed to compose myself in those couple of seconds and think what to say, to thank everyone and say the right things.

RICHARD: Then I shouted, 'Thank you Collaborators, we love you!' I just wanted to let our fans know how much their support had meant to us.

JAMIE: We felt so grateful that the public had voted for us. We later found out that in the final we had won 26.5 per cent of the votes and Lucy had got 17 per cent, so we were still very clearly in front. Never in a million years did we think that was going to happen.

MATT: It just didn't seem real. You forget about absolutely everything else for a few moments and then suddenly they said, 'So are you going to perform again for us?' I'd completely forgotten about the winner's encore, but we were all like, 'YES!'

RICHARD: I was so dazed from the shock of winning that I sang the wrong opening line. I recited the lyric from the first audition, so instead of singing, 'Stars in your multitude', I sang, 'There, out in the darkness'. I suddenly thought, *Richard, you are singing the wrong words!* There is a moment where you can see I look to Michael… and we share a wry smile. I thought, *What am I doing?* Then I thought, *Who is gonna really care, WE HAVE WON!* When Matt follows my wrong lyric with his correct lyric, it makes no sense but no one really cottoned on. No one ever commented on it after either. It didn't matter.

MICHAEL: That performance was so emotional. When Richard finished and Matt started, I just touched Richard's hand and smiled at him. I just wanted to reassure him it really didn't matter. It was funny though.

RICHARD: You can tell how much more relaxed we all are because when it came to Michael's solo, I still had my arm around him!

MATT: We were all shaken by what had just happened. No one minded about the wrong lyrics; we'd done it. We sang the song, did the same routine and walked forward, then hit the key change and all this confetti started falling down…

RICHARD: …It was all in our mouths and I was breathing it in while singing, but none of that mattered. We had won…

MATT: …and the crowd was going mad. This was what I had been dreaming about since I was a little boy. What a moment.

Tom: Another standing ovation. Not that I'm counting. But for the record, it was.

JAMIE: I was still crying when the main show wrapped and then suddenly we were live on *Britain's Got More Talent*. Stephen Mulhern turned to me first and said, 'At least they are tears of joy... but look, not only the Royal Variety Performance, but also £250,000. What are you going to buy?' I hadn't even thought about the money. For me it was never about the money, it was about doing something I believed in, and I believe 100 per cent in Collabro. We hadn't really entered *Britain's Got Talent* for the money – how could you predict that we would go all the way through and win £250,000? But I'm not going to lie: our £50,000 share each was very welcome! We'd all had long periods when money was really tight. I answered with the first instinctive thing that came into my head and said, 'I dunno, I'm gonna do something nice for my mum.'

MATT: That was one of the best moments ever. I can honestly say until Stephen mentioned the prize money I hadn't even remembered there was a cash prize, or for that matter that we were now going to be playing at the Royal Variety Performance. We had just been so focused on winning. Before *Britain's Got Talent* I was at a really low point with money. I was overdrawn and really struggling, so to hear him ask about the prize money was amazing. I remember thinking, *I can afford to live now.*

TOM: Absolutely! I couldn't agree more. The prizes – the Royal Variety, all of that – you don't think about them at all, you just think about winning. So when Stephen asked that question you can see me standing next to Jamie thinking, *Brilliant! Now I can pay my rent.*

JAMIE: When Stephen turned to Tom, you can see we start to get our composure back and we thanked the other acts and the people who'd voted for us. It was such a whirlwind though: you are told you've won this massive competition, you know your life will change and then suddenly BANG! There's a microphone in your face and you are being asked all these questions... when it's all you can do to keep standing up straight from the emotion.

RICHARD: Then they brought us a silver tray of champagne and invited our family and friends up onstage.

JAMIE: At which point I saw my mum and started crying all over again! I think part of the emotion coming out was thinking of other people who couldn't see what was happening. For example, Nana would have been so proud of Collabro. She died before I really started singing, which is so sad because she would have been so excited by everything that has happened. Unfortunately she had an unhealthy life – she smoked forever. You did in those days, in working-class Yorkshire families. She would have dined out on the success. Some of my biggest supporters haven't been here to see our success because they have passed away.

MATT: After the show they wanted to talk to us upstairs. Peter Andre and Chico were there and Peter came over and said 'Well done'. Ant and Dec talked to us for ages, which I still found weird – they are so famous and yet so nice. Then loads of producers came over saying 'Well done' and poured us more champagne!

RICHARD: I just wanted to party! The way we got treated was just fantastic; they were continuously topping us up with champagne. That was great. Then we did another interview with Stephen for *Britain's Got More Talent* where we answered viewers' questions and I expressed how much I loved drinking – even beginning to list my favourite tipples – until Michael shut me up! I was just so, so happy.

MICHAEL: We finished the questions and then had a dance. We didn't get too drunk because we knew we had lots of interviews the next day but it was just so nice. Everyone came up to congratulate us. One of the contestants, the violinist Lettuce Rowbotham, said, 'Woo-hoo! Well done! Have some champagne!' Lucy Kay was being lovely – of course – and Jack Pack too, who were obviously gutted.

MATT: Meanwhile I couldn't get on Facebook or Twitter because my phone had gone into meltdown.

TOM: The *Britain's Got More Talent* interviews took a little while but we were served champagne for the whole duration so no one minded!

JAMIE: All the time we were thinking, *We want to go and see our families*.

MATT: We had just done these interviews with Stephen and, like Jamie says, we were desperate to see everyone. When we walked through the doors into the holding area in the canteen at Fountain Studios where they were all waiting, the cheers and noise were deafening.

That was probably the most emotional moment of the whole *Britain's Got Talent* experience.

JAMIE: The sound when we walked in to the holding area was just a massive wall of noise. Everyone was there: family, friends, producers, production staff, it was so, so good – a brilliant feeling. What a fantastic way to end the night, with all those people who had supported us over all those years. Perfect.

TOM: That was a great party; we were all so proud, so excited, so tired, but the champagne was flowing and everyone was just so happy. It was a fantastic feeling, it really was.

JAMIE: I was in a state of shock. I had a feeling that everyone we had known in our lives was watching that final: people from primary school, all of our family, our old friends that don't really stay in touch any more, they were all watching the final because they knew we were on. And now we had won it.

In between the celebrating and chatting, sipping champagne and hugging family, I just kept thinking, *We have won* Britain's Got Talent!

We had done it.

We had won *Britain's Got Talent*.

CHAPTER 6

THE DEBUT ALBUM AND LIFE AS THE WINNERS OF *BRITAIN'S GOT TALENT*

MATT: Waking up the day after your group has won *Britain's Got Talent* is a very odd moment. You open your eyes and suddenly all these memories flood back; you remember what happened, you wonder what will happen next and your brain is swamped with so many thoughts and feelings.

MICHAEL: I actually slept on Jamie's sofa in Shepherd's Bush that night. Oh, the glamour. I think I got to sleep around 5am. The car was coming to pick us up for a day of interviews at 7am.

TOM: I was still moving house! When we'd been in the party the night before, one of the production team took us to one side and said, 'Listen, guys, well done, amazing achievement. You have a lot of interviews tomorrow, so enjoy tonight for what it is!' When he said that I thought, *Oh my God! I have got to move house tomorrow!* In the end, my family did most of the packing and moving. I think I eventually got home about 6pm and moved a couple of boxes, but they'd basically done everything for me.

MICHAEL: To give you an idea of how mad that first day after the final was (and indeed the first few weeks!), this is what I wrote in my diary:

'Woke up early to get to Sony for hair and make-up, ready for the day ahead! We headed to the Royal Park Hotel in Regent Street for a photo shoot then over to Buckingham Palace gardens for more photos, then a quick radio interview with Matt Edmondson on Radio 1 in the middle of a photo shoot ☺ We then had two sit down 'round' interviews with all the big newspapers who absolutely grilled us which was scary, but we've got each other so no need to worry. I'm so tired but still loving every moment! I can't believe last night happened, the dream is becoming reality! We finished up about 5pm and headed home to watch the BGT Final back – SO SURREAL! Must get early to bed! Can't wait until tomorrow for *Good Morning Britain, Lorraine, This Morning* and then a *Heat* magazine shoot!! Night ☺ x'

JAMIE: That extract from Michael's diary pretty much sums it up perfectly. It was all a bit of a daze, to be honest. We were being taken everywhere and shipped in cars all over the place. We were really enjoying it, just trying to ride the wave.

RICHARD: We'd all celebrated after winning but were quite sensible because we knew about the workload the day after. Me being me, I thought, *We have just won Britain's Got Talent, PARTY!* All my family and mates were there, my girlfriend too, so I had a great time. I lived off adrenalin and excitement until about midday on the

Sunday, but then it started to catch up on me and I was absolutely shattered for the rest of the day.

JAMIE: Although it was a very busy day, I loved it. I just felt so proud. It was a really good feeling to think that I had finally done something like this, that I could say to people, 'Look what I have done, this is us, we did this!' I received hundreds of messages that day – our phones were constantly going off. I was overwhelmed.

RICHARD: In the week that followed, the work just ramped up and up and up. We did hundreds of interviews. The funny thing was, one day that week when I was in central London, I opened my wallet and I only had £5 in there. Just £5 to my name even though we'd just won *Britain's Got Talent.* The prize money hadn't yet cleared in all of our accounts so we were all still skint. I looked for a cashpoint but when I got there I'd left my cash card at home so even if there was any money in my account I couldn't get it! I had to phone Mum and ask her if she'd transfer some money into my account so I could go into the nearby bank, draw it out and afford the train ticket home. It was either that or I'd have to go busking! When the prize money did arrive, I actually wanted to see that number, £50,000, in black on my bank statement. That was a nice thing to see, to say the least!

On a practical level, one big difference that I feel daily is the financial benefit. I don't need to worry about the bus fare into town. I can take my girlfriend out for dinner. That is the biggest change, not having to worry about the small things and just being able to live life. Best of all, I am making the money by singing. I can't begin to tell you how good that feels.

TOM: Back in the week after the win, we noticed that a 'meeting with Syco, Thursday,' was scheduled in our diary. We thought, *What is that about?* We assumed it would just be a 'well done' chat, really.

MATT: So we all went to the Syco office for the meeting, even though we had no idea why it was scheduled in. We went in, shook all their hands and then sat down in front of a man called Sonny Takhar, who is one of the key figures at Syco and a hugely influential man in the record industry. Then he said, 'Right, this is what we are thinking will work on the album...'

JAMIE: We all thought, *Did he just say something about an album?* It was never a given that we'd get a record deal. It certainly wasn't a part of the prize for winning. We obviously hoped someone might want to talk to us about a deal but that was all we had hoped for: some initial chats. So I wasn't ready for him to say that.

MICHAEL: Then he said they were thinking of starting with a certain selection of songs... and I was barely able to follow him, I was still thinking, *Did he just say something about an album?*

TOM: I heard his words but was thinking, *Have I missed a couple of steps here?* We wouldn't dare be so arrogant to presume that we'd got a record deal with anyone, never mind with Syco.

RICHARD: Me too – I was stunned. At this point I had to interrupt politely and say, 'Sorry, sorry, can I just stop you for one second, are you actually saying we are going to do an album?' Sonny just smiled and said, 'Yes, you are now signed to Syco along with

One Direction, Susan Boyle and Il Divo.' That was just the most ridiculous realisation. None of us saw that coming.

MATT: Someone brought in more champagne and then Sonny said, 'Now it's the fun part, let's start listening to some of the initial ideas for the album track-listing, which you will start recording next week.' I thought, *Oh my God, this is just getting ridiculous now.* I looked at Sonny and behind his desk on the wall were all these platinum discs awarded for millions of record sales to bands like 1D, Susan Boyle, Il Divo, Little Mix, and now we were on the same label. It was mad.

JAMIE: They were so nice in welcoming us into the fold. They were amazing. Syco don't sign people unless they think they are going to do well so that was a massive, massive boost. The songs put forward were great, too. There were the big musical theatre numbers but also a couple of more surprising choices. 'Secrets' by One Republic and 'All of Me' by John Legend ended up on the album but with a Collabro twist. I think that's a really exciting blend.

MICHAEL: We went through the album song choices and I loved all the ideas. I couldn't wait to go to the recording studio – it was all starting the very next week. If we'd not won that show, I really think I would've been back at the petrol station that week. Certainly I'd have had to get money in from somewhere, even if the band had attracted lots of interest from the final. Instead we were sipping champagne in Syco's head office then going to a top studio to start recording an album that was going to be released by one of the biggest record labels in the world.

JAMIE: We recorded the album at a really plush residential studio in Woking. It was such a nice place to work; Syco had really done us proud.

MICHAEL: The day before the album sessions started, we were invited to the *Walking On Sunshine* movie premiere in central London. This was a totally new experience for all of us: there was champagne in the cinema; we went to the after-show party and met the stars of the film as well as famous guests like Emma Thompson and then had a bit of a dance. We all left at about 11pm because we were recording the next day.

RICHARD: My mum had bought me an hour in a small local studio for my birthday one time, but I had zero experience in terms of the level of the studio in Woking. It was really cool: it had tennis courts, a swimming pool, games rooms, there was even a puppy called Dexter who was just the cutest thing you have ever seen. It was a really nice place to be.

TOM: I had previously been in a few local bands around Lincoln and I had done a little bit of studio but not a huge amount. We recorded a few short EPs where we sang in a local recording studio, but that was usually either a shed or somebody's toilet that had been renovated into a studio. This place was a full on, top of the range residential recording studio.

JAMIE: I had done some limited studio work before but not on this scale. It was a great experience. The album sessions would turn out to be quick, exciting, enjoyable and stressful all at the same time. We only had nine days to record ten songs but we hadn't even arranged or learnt the parts yet because our diaries had been completely rammed with PR and promotion. Although we had the list of potential songs, there was not a single moment free when we might've got to a rehearsal studio to work out arrangements or even learn the lyrics to the new songs. We arranged and learnt the parts with the vocal arranger and producer in the morning, then recorded it in the afternoon until late at night. It was pretty brutal.

MICHAEL: The album was quite intense but I was just so happy to be there, so excited to be recording an album, it really would've taken a big problem to knock me off my stride. I just felt really lucky. Then Matt got ill...

MATT: You can imagine how excited we all were about the album sessions. So you can also imagine how I felt when I became really ill. Then – disaster! – I found out I had laryngitis. I'd been home to see my family for the first time since the first audition and I went out for a drink in the evening. I think I must've picked up the bug from a dirty glass. The night before I was supposed to go back to London on the train, I said to my mum, 'I am starting to feel really ill, my glands are swollen, I am not feeling good at all, but I am supposed to be recording tomorrow.' I was absolutely gutted.

JAMIE: It was already a demanding recording schedule and when we found out how ill Matt was the nerves were starting to go wild! We really wanted to make this album something special.

MATT: I went back to London to see a top laryngologist the next day and he put a camera down my throat. You could see on this little monitor that my vocal cords were really swollen. He had a look, shook his head and said, 'Matt, absolutely no singing for a week, I'm afraid. Under no circumstances. NO SINGING WHATSOEVER.' He was very clear about that and said I risked serious damage if I didn't do as he recommended. This was coming from one of the top guys in Harley Street. It was a massive kick in the teeth.

RICHARD: When Matt got laryngitis it was a nightmare. We couldn't delay the recording – there was an album release date to meet and all sorts of promotional work lined up – so we needed to record the album. I was so worried about Matt and the schedule. What would happen if he couldn't come in to sing at all?

MATT: Like all the lads, I was getting stressed – this was our first album and I couldn't sing. I had to ring the producer of the album – the brilliant Graham Stack – and say, 'I shouldn't even be talking to you, I should be texting you, but I'm afraid I am not allowed to sing for a week.' He was great and said, 'Don't even come to the studio, Matt. Stay away completely, just rest and get better.'

MICHAEL: I felt for Matt because he was missing out on the experience. We had to crack on without him, we were performing the songs, working on the album, relaxing around the complex; it was really harsh for him to be ill like that.

MATT: I just had to stay at home but eventually I did go back a couple of days earlier than I should have because I felt my voice was coming back. I went to Woking and said, 'Can I just try and sing?' They put me in the booth and I sang through one of the songs but it was still not quite there, so they told me to get a good night's sleep and try again the next day.

Thankfully, by the next morning I had fully recovered. There was a really nice moment when I was singing one of my first lines and the musical director Richard just buzzed the link that allows the control desk to talk to the singing booth and he said, 'And he's back! Good to have you back with us, Matt!'

What a relief! Mind you, then I had to do all my parts for ten songs in just two days! When I recorded 'With You' from *Ghost*, I was encouraged to remember someone I had lost, so I just thought of Grandad the whole time I was singing that vocal. The boys were so supportive the whole time; what a brilliant way for them to react.

RICHARD: The band got very close during the album sessions. Like those early Pontins dates, this was another point where we spent a whole week in each others' pockets. We worked really hard and also relaxed together, so over the course of that week we cemented our friendship even more.

TOM: Yes, it was really good. Like a lot of bands we much prefer performing but recording the album was enjoyable too – it was a new experience. It was stressful to get it all done, especially with Matt being so ill, but it was really enjoyable.

By now we'd invented various nicknames for the band, which was just a bit of fun. Jamie is 'The Giraffe' because of his height and frame. Richard is 'The Seal'. He was going to be a bear or rhino because of his size but then he did a brilliant seal impression so that was that. Michael is 'The Peacock' because he always takes the longest to get ready. Matt is 'The Bush Monkey' because of his 'cheeky chappie' nature. Finally, I am 'The Lion Cub' because I'm a bit quirky (and small and cute, apparently).

JAMIE: With the album sessions finally completed, it was back to more promotion, public appearances and getting ourselves ready for the album launch in the summer. The interest in us because we had won *Britain's Got Talent* was huge. I think winning was important; it has given us a real kick. I know acts have come second and done incredibly well – Susan Boyle, for example! – but coming first has definitely been a big boost, in my opinion. It's opened so many doors.

MICHAEL: There was no let-up in the workload but we were just having the best time, even though the hours were incredibly long.

RICHARD: Syco asked us to do a few so-called 'touch-ups' and some more recording for the album to perfect it. In typical Collabro style – always wondering how we can improve – we thought, *Is this a good thing? Obviously they want to make it better but are we not doing a good enough job?* Of course now we know it's fairly standard practice. Albums get polished all the time, it's all a natural part of honing the record.

MATT: We were more than happy to keep working on the album. It meant there was a slight delay in the release, but even though that frustrated a few fans, we preferred to get the record right rather than just rush it out for the sake of it.

RICHARD: It's funny how certain little incidents make you realise how much your life has changed. When we were touching up the album, we went to a place called Music Bank to listen to some of the backing tracks. On one of our breaks, we went down to a nearby cafe for lunch and the guy behind the counter was asking us what we did. When we said we were working at Music Bank he said, 'Wow, you guys must be really famous to book in there!' When he found out about winning *Britain's Got Talent*, he said, 'Oh my God! I know you guys!' Then he was really quite taken aback. That was odd, to get that reaction.

MATT: After a few amendments, we got to the point where Syco said the album was spot-on and signed it off.

JAMIE: That was in July. We were also doing loads of gigs, festivals and appearances – it was so hectic, but also great fun! I enjoyed the Wimbledon preview party just before the tennis championships started. That was at Kensington Palace Gardens on my birthday. We got a bit trashed, to be fair. It was a really good day.

MICHAEL: We did an *OK!* magazine shoot around then too. It felt like a big deal because it's such a high profile publication.

RICHARD: We would occasionally get a few hours off which would be nice, but most of the time I was dashing up to London on the train to work. Eventually it became apparent that I needed to move to the capital, because being in Brighton was holding us back a bit. I had to get a train everywhere and I would often be late because trains are rubbish. It was taxing on the band. So I got a flat in a skyscraper in east London, floor to ceiling windows, absolutely beautiful. I know lots of people who live in really grimy student accommodation, so I felt incredibly lucky at 20 (I am the baby of the group even though I don't look it!) to be in this fabulous London pad in the sky.

JAMIE: Matt and Richard hadn't really lived away from home until the group kicked off so I think that was a new and exciting experience for them. They are lucky though, because when I think back to all the dingy dives I've lived in over the years...

RICHARD: When I moved out, my parents were really emotional and upset. It had all happened so quickly and they wanted to share the whole experience. I had gone from living there all the time to moving out completely. A lot of my friends have moved out to a flat in Hove and see their parents every day. Others have gone to university and see their parents some weekends, and then obviously during the holidays they move back home. I never did that; I was just living at home one minute, then Collabro kicked off and I moved out to London. When the time came, I wasn't surprised that my mum got very emotional, but I found out later that my dad cried too. He's not the type to show his emotions too easily so he must've been really upset. Mum said she asked him what was the matter and he just said, 'I don't want Richard to move away.' Yet even though they knew the job would take me away from home, they still supported me 100 per cent because that's how brilliant they are.

MATT: Same with my parents. It was so hard moving away; I loved living with them and being in Carlisle. They didn't want me to be so far away but at the same time they were really happy for me that the band was taking off. They're just amazing parents.

MICHAEL: One really fun perk of winning the show is getting invited to loads of film premieres. We went to the premieres for films such as *Guardians of the Galaxy* (we stood next to Vin Diesel on the red carpet), *Pudsey* and *Jersey Boys* – there were lots of parties and invitations to events, it was just a total rollercoaster.

JAMIE: Ahead of the album launch we performed at Stratford's Westfield shopping centre, and we pushed the button on the Lottery Show, which was surreal. It was a non-stop barrage of new and exciting things to be involved in.

MATT: We appeared on QVC just before the album came out. We sang on that shopping channel and in the two minutes it took us to perform 'Bring Him Home' and chat briefly, QVC had sold all their copies.

TOM: We did a series of CD signings to promote the album too. That was great because it was perhaps the first time we'd really had a good chance to meet the fans up close.

MICHAEL: Yes, I really enjoyed those. It was hard to start a conversation because there were so many people and we didn't really have much time. We were so grateful for the fans voting for us and then coming along to support the album. I did find it a little strange that some of the fans were shaking when I spoke to them – it was quite a new thing for me to get used to. I didn't really understand it; I kind of knew what was going on but the fact it was me didn't really make sense, if you know what I mean?

JAMIE: The week of the album's release was just mad! We had a radio tour to promote the record, we met fans and we had some performances too. Then at the end of the week we had a charity show for RNLI Lifeboat charity in Rhyl and it was during our journey home in the car afterwards when the new official album charts were being announced on Radio 1.

TOM: We knew that sales were going well because you are given a so-called 'midweek' position, but a lot can change in the second half of the week. Plus, Ed Sheeran was at Number 1 and his album was already one of the biggest selling records of the year.

MATT: Like Tom says, we were getting updates all week. It had been climbing and it was also at Number 1 on iTunes, so it was looking good, but we still wanted to hear it on the Official Chart. We were travelling back on the motorway with the car radio on and then the DJ said something like, 'Let's see who has knocked Ed Sheeran off the top spot,' and then he started playing 'Let It Go'! We went mental! We were clapping and cheering like mad, the car must have been shaking down the motorway!

RICHARD: That was a crazy day. We had just performed to thousands of people and were all a little bit knackered. Then Radio 1 came on and announced we were Number 1! I thought, *Oh my God this is amazing; this is truly awesome. We have a Number 1 album.* That is a whole other level. Winning *Britain's Got Talent* was amazing but to get a Number 1 album in the mainstream charts with musical theatre was something else.

MICHAEL: There has always been such a high degree of separation between classical music and pop, hence why they've got the classical charts and the mainstream charts, so I think it is really exciting to blur those lines with Collabro.

THE DEBUT ALBUM AND LIFE AS THE WINNERS OF *BRITAIN'S GOT TALENT*

JAMIE: I couldn't agree more. Selling enough records to get to Number 1 is an incredible achievement for any band. For me, to do that with musical theatre is something I am so proud of. To even get a musical theatre group played on Radio 1 is not easy. What Collabro aspires to do is take musical theatre out of the classical scene and bring it to the forefront of the mainstream music industry. For something like our music to get Number 1 in the actual charts, not the classical charts but the Official Top 40 Album Chart, is mad. Someone called us a cross between Il Divo and One Direction and I think that's very complimentary: they are obviously both hugely successful and fantastic groups so I'll take that!

RICHARD: I sometimes think of the album hitting Number 1 and then wonder whether that has happened.

MATT: Being shot into this sort of limelight is super-exciting, obviously, and it is something that we had all strived for over a long period of time. It is interesting too when you start to get recognised; that is a whole new dynamic in your life that takes some getting used to.

MICHAEL: From the time after the first *Britain's Got Talent* audition when those audience members saw us afterwards in the entrance hall, to the 1D fans cheering us on, to our own signings and meeting fans, I feel incredibly privileged that people recognise us and want to support us the way that they do. Around the time of the album launch I was walking through central London and some fans spotted me outside Planet Hollywood. They approached me and were really nice; they got a few selfies and chatted away. How can you not find that exciting?

TOM: As perhaps the most introverted member of the band, I was a little apprehensive about how winning the show might affect my life in terms of being recognised. However, I can honestly say that it is almost always entirely pleasant, not least because most of the people are really respectful and nice. If they see me somewhere they politely ask for a photo and chat away, enthusing about the album or a gig they have seen. They're just really nice people. We really want to make that effort to spend time with the fans, so, for example, if there are fans waiting outside in the cold after a gig, how can you not find the time to go and speak with them? We want to go and see them and say hello and thank them for supporting us. I would hate to be the artist that does their show and then just zooms off in a car as quickly as possible. We want to show our gratitude for all that they have done for us.

MATT: Totally. Our fans are amazing. We love them – they are great. Right back from when that very first *Britain's Got Talent* audition was screened they have backed us all the way – after that very first audition when I was sat at home with my iPad, I couldn't get on-line because we'd instantly got all these new followers. The fan base has just kept getting bigger and bigger and bigger. Our fans are unusual too in the sense that a lot of them are not even on Twitter or Facebook. We do have our share of older fans, yet they still follow us, support us and sometimes that can be a really big inconvenience or expense in their lives but they do it anyway. We really love the fact that people will write and ask for an autograph, so we will spend as much time as we can with fans because at the end of the day we wouldn't be doing any of this without them.

THE DEBUT ALBUM AND LIFE AS THE WINNERS OF *BRITAIN'S GOT TALENT*

TOM: During *Britain's Got Talent*, we got a lot of scrutiny from some of the Bars And Melody fans, many of whom said they have ten times the amount of views and followers on social media, but we are proud that a lot of our audience is from an older generation. It's nice that we have both fan bases. Musical theatre isn't in popular culture that much at the moment, so to also have people following us on social media like they follow One Direction or Union J is incredible and it means we are helping to introduce the younger generation to this genre of music.

RICHARD: Our first *Britain's Got Talent* audition was very different and it seems that it has inspired quite a few people. We each get messages all the time from fans saying they have given something a go because they were inspired by that audition. It is so heartwarming to read and really inspires me in return. What a lovely thing to say to us.

Every artist in the industry has an important role, however successful or not they are – and we are aware we are just starting out – because you never know who is listening. Some people may listen and say it is nice background music, but other people may listen to every single word and some songs change people's lives.

JAMIE: Our fans are very respectful. They approach us politely. They often know musical theatre and even if they are new to that genre they have done their homework and really got into it. It never ceases to amaze me when they queue up for hours to meet us at signings or stand outside after gigs. We never forget these are the people who voted for us to win *Britain's Got Talent*. They are just fantastic. How can we ever thank them for that?

MICHAEL: This one guy on Twitter has taken a song for each of us from the album and created these amazing films comprised of all the clips he can find of us. It's just so amazing to me that someone would spend that amount of time making that for us. Those are the fans that make it all worthwhile because, although we absolutely love Collabro and wouldn't change anything that's happened, if we are ever over-tired or anxious about something to do with the band or just struggling on a particular day, those are the people who lift our spirits and make us go again.

RICHARD: I have found it so fantastic. There has probably been only one moment where it kind of freaked me out a bit. It was the first time I struggled with the whole fame side of it. I went back home one Saturday and it was a friend's birthday so I turned up and this person said, 'Hey, superstar, how are you, celebrity?' I thought, *What? What is she talking about?* That just didn't sit well with me at all; I was most uncomfortable. Then I was introduced to various people at the party and it was all about Collabro – I get that, I can see that it was news and people wanted to know, but I was getting bombarded with all these questions. I was just really uneasy with the celebrity tag, especially in my private life. It was really strange and I didn't know how to cope with it, so I just needed to get out of there.

As I mentioned in my individual chapter, I don't like people to judge me before they've actually got to know me. Maybe this is a throwback from when people looked at this overweight kid and made a judgement on sight. I dunno, maybe I'm reading too much into it, but I do know that the party and that reaction made me realise how some people will make a snap judgement without ever really knowing me. That's quite an odd feeling. I'm not complaining, I'm just being really honest and saying that took me a little while to get used to. I would never call myself a celebrity. We are professional singers in a group; there's a crucial difference.

MATT: It is fair to say that in certain circumstances you no longer have elements of your own life. But you need to keep a perspective on what is happening. I was told by David McNeill, my theatre director in Cumbria, to never forget the people on the way up because you will have to pass them on the way down. That has stuck with me, so I enjoy the movie premieres, parties, radio appearances and all the perks, and I will always try to be nice and polite to people, and stay hard working and punctual. It's simple common courtesy really, but I think it makes a difference.

RICHARD: I spoke to a famous film director at one premiere and I asked him if he had any advice on how to process this landslide of publicity that we were experiencing. He said to me, 'I know it sounds really rubbish but there will come a time when you are so tired and emotionally exhausted that you will get upset and you will be really bummed out. Then you will wonder why on earth you are upset when you have the career you always dreamed of. Just step back, don't be hard on yourself, try to find time for a break, you will get used to it.' That was fantastic advice. I think that party in Brighton was maybe my time to be a bit confused. I think the pressure of everything was really getting on top of me and I didn't know how to deal with it all. Fortunately – and just like the film director said – now I'm far more accustomed to the lifestyle and that makes it even more enjoyable.

MICHAEL: I've found the whole fame element thoroughly enjoyable. However, for a completely different reason there was one underlying anxiety when the band started that I'd like to tell you about. For a long time I was worried I was going to be cut out of this group... because everyone is so good. Right back from when I turned up at the rehearsals in January after they'd already offered me the job, I was still thinking, *They might change their mind.* For a long time I felt almost too nervous to enjoy what was happening. For example, when we went to the recording studio for the first time, I still didn't really believe that I had my rightful place in the band. I vividly remember standing in the booth by the mic and feeling so nervous. Some of the parts that we had agreed and arranged had been swapped, so I was then worried it was because they maybe thought my voice wasn't right for certain parts. That wasn't the case, of course, but it does reflect this on-going anxiety I was having.

It wasn't until we appeared on *Sunday Night At The Palladium* with Jason Manford that I first felt like I deserved my place in this group. Jason was really relaxed and made us feel so welcome; the performance with him was great fun and I really enjoyed the whole day. I could see my family in the second row of the Royal Circle; I spotted them because my sister was wearing a sequinned dress. That was the first time, literally, that I felt like I deserved to be here. I have never felt more confident and relaxed in a performance so that was the nicest feeling for me, finally, to feel that way.

RICHARD: I think if you are not an arrogant person, there are always going to be times when you might feel like Michael did. I wasn't sure about fans giving me a lot of attention and waiting outside in the rain for me to sign a bit of paper and maybe get a selfie. I just thought, *Do I deserve this? Really? Do I deserve these people to* *really appreciate me this much when only last winter I was up a scaffolding doing a bit of painting?* That's honestly how I felt at first. However, I get it now. I know that the fans enjoy themselves, that they want to do that and I can only say I am privileged that this is the case and can't thank them enough.

JAMIE: Another obvious repercussion of becoming a known face after winning *Britain's Got Talent* is that your personal life can sometimes be scrutinised. We are obviously reviewed for our singing and performing but there is an extra layer of your private life being looked at too. That's not a problem, if you don't want any public recognition then maybe going on *Britain's Got Talent* isn't a good idea. You need to be realistic.

RICHARD: Part of the vulnerability of being in Collabro is that we are known for our five personalities. When I was aspiring to be a musical theatre singer, I always saw myself as being an actor performing a role in a song. I never saw myself performing as *myself*. Even when I busked, I was a caricature of myself, whereas now I am just myself so it can be quite scary going on stage. There is no role, no character to hide behind. That takes some getting used to.

JAMIE: Most relevantly to me, one newspaper ran a piece saying that I had 'come out'. I never came out. Mainly because I had never denied I was gay, for a start! Another magazine asked me whether I was gay or not and shortly after, we gave an exclusive to *The Sun*, whose writer Dan Wooton wrote a very sensitive, very delicate article about the subject, which I really appreciated. He pointed out that my family has always known I was gay, so have all of my friends, and how it has always been treated like a normal thing in my family because it is a normal thing. Then this other newspaper ran a piece saying I had revealed I was gay and had come out. That just wasn't the case. That surprised me, in this day and age.

MICHAEL: There are other stand-out moments: Brighton Pride was massive for all of us; we absolutely loved it. There were 50,000 people in front of us – the biggest crowd we have performed to – and they all went absolutely wild.

TOM: Especially when they were all singing along to 'Let It Go'. For the last lyric of that song, 'The cold never bothered me anyway', well, I don't think Jamie actually sang any of that, he just held the microphone out and 50,000 shouted the words back at us. That was an incredible feeling.

MATT: Because I did the pubs and clubs circuit I'm used to turning up to a gig and finding a pretty plain or even dingy venue. So I am still in that phase where we turn up to shows and can't believe how amazing every venue is.

RICHARD: As the rugby player in the group, you probably won't be surprised to hear that one of my favourite Collabro moments was when we were asked to sing at Jonny Wilkinson's testimonial; that was crazy!

MATT: Oh my God, absolutely. We got to sing with Alfie Boe, one of the best vocalists in the world, in front of Prince Harry. How cool is that?

RICHARD: You can imagine: there I was, singing with Alfie Boe, my all-time hero in terms of playing Valjean, performing at a testimonial for one of my all-time favourite rugby players. I literally could not be happier. That night was really special. I bought Jonny Wilkinson a whisky and then met all these famous rugby players, my heroes. They got Jonny Wilkinson to sign my invite! It is just unbelievable, the things that are happening to us because of Collabro.

JAMIE: I still had a great night even though I'm not a sports person. I don't know a lot about rugby but I did know that Jonny Wilkinson was the man who kicked the winning try that won us the 2003 World Cup. All I kept thinking about was that Prince Harry was there! It was a really special night. Along with Alfie Boe and Laura White we performed 'World In Union' and then Jonny Wilkinson requested his favourite song, 'That's Life', which we did as well. To show you how Collabro really takes every event seriously, we paid for a musical director to rehearse us and prepare that performance, even though it was only likely to be two songs.

MICHAEL: My sister is just the biggest Jonny Wilkinson fan and she pleaded with me to get a selfie with him. I was really awkward about that on the night but eventually I plucked up the courage and said to Jonny, 'This is really cringey, but my sister is in love with you so can I get a selfie to show her please?' He laughed and was really good about it. And yes, I got the selfie.

RICHARD: I still play rugby when I can. I've turned up for a few photo shoots with a battle scar or scratch from a game of rugby. At first the boys and management would say, 'Oh my God, you've got this massive scratch!' but I would always just say, 'Oh, they can

Photoshop it out if they really need to. Or better still, leave it in!'
Now I think people know that it's part of who I am and hopefully
they may even like it. This group has always been about changing
people's opinions so why try and pretend you are something you
are not. Collabro is not about putting up a false front.

TOM: We also sang with Michael Ball at a West End Heroes charity
concert. He's a musical theatre legend. I would never have imagined
we would get the chance to sing with that calibre of performer.
People like Michael Ball and Alfie Boe are so respected in the field
that we love, so to be alongside them on stage is just so fortunate.

MATT: We've also performed at the International Wine Challenge
awards; we sang with Rob Brydon and I could see Julie Walters sat
directly in front of us, to the left was Mick Jagger and to the right
was Stephen Fry. I was singing and thinking to myself, How did we
get to this point? I just cherish every moment like that.

JAMIE: We've had some incredible moments since winning the show
but one of my personal favourites was when we were asked to
surprise Simon Cowell and sing at his private birthday party. I have
never been so nervous, even before our first audition for *Britain's
Got Talent!* It was this tiny little Italian restaurant and there were
only about 40 people invited. There was no fancy PA system;
there were just a few little speakers on the wall. Ordinarily a gig
of that size is quite demanding because the audience is right in
your face, there's nowhere to hide and it can be quite intimidating.
Well, on that night the audience was like a Who's Who of British
entertainment, so as well as Simon Cowell we were singing in front
of Cheryl Cole, David Walliams, Amanda Holden, Louis Walsh,

Alesha Dixon, Sinitta, Philip Green, Sonny Takhar from Syco – the list went on and on. I was shaking, I can't tell you.

MATT: That was just like the audition all over again! As Jamie said, it was a surprise for Simon so we were hiding upstairs by the toilets and at one point Alesha walked towards us so we had to hide, laughing as we did so.

JAMIE: We sang 'Bring Him Home' and 'With You' which is Simon's favourite track on the album. Afterwards, Simon came up and shook our hands and said, 'That was phenomenal, thank you.' That was a really special night.

TOM: We got a standing ovation from everyone, which included the four *Britain's Got Talent* judges so I am counting that in my tally!

MICHAEL: I don't want to speak for the other boys but perhaps the most obvious stand-out performance, certainly in terms of what it meant to us all personally and in the context of this band's career, was when we performed the curtain call at the actual West End production of *Les Misérables* at The Queen's Theatre. That was pretty special.

JAMIE: Oh my God, you are so right. That was the week of the album's release and they didn't actually tell anyone in the audience. We were so excited when we found out it was happening. You have to remember, that musical was effectively Collabro's common denominator; we had all loved that show, adored those lyrics, played various parts, been to see it on stage, watched the DVDs, and performed those songs at *Britain's Got Talent*. *Les Misérables* is just a part of us as people and a part of this band. In some senses, being asked to sing at the *Les Misérables* curtain call meant we had all come full circle.

MATT: On the night itself, we were standing at the back of the Queen's Theatre stage in total darkness; no one out in the audience knew we were there. Then suddenly the lights went up and you could hear people murmuring, wondering what was going on.

RICHARD: Peter Lockyer, who was playing Valjean, came on and said, 'Thank you very much for this evening, ladies and gentlemen. Now, we have got something a little bit different for you, five boys who took the nation by storm in winning *Britain's Got Talent...*'

MICHAEL: I was physically shaking at this point. It just meant so much to us to be singing in that theatre.

MATT: Then we walked out into view and the crowd went absolutely mad. It was overwhelming. Of all the stages and theatres for that to happen, to get that response at the *Les Misérables* theatre... WOW!

RICHARD: The whole place just erupted and went absolutely crazy. That is the most scared I have ever been on stage. It is something from the bucket list – for all of us to perform on a West End stage just after one of the biggest shows of all-time. That was an educated audience, they know their musical theatre, so to get that reaction was a huge boost.

TOM: There was a woman in the front row and when we walked out you could clearly hear her saying, 'Oh my God, it's Collabro, oh my God, it's Collabro!' over and over again.

JAMIE: We sang 'Bring Him Home' and 'Stars' and got a standing ovation from the whole audience. I have never been so proud; it was amazing. What a night to remember.

My mum knew what she was talking about all those years ago when she was encouraging that little kid with his music homework. She told me then, and it is utterly true, there is a difference between people who sing in tune brilliantly and people who make you tingle when they perform. I would like to think that Collabro sing technically very well but also that we make that connection, that almost unquantifiable emotional link with the music and the audience, that certain performers have. Maybe that's what the audience felt that night at the Queen's Theatre. I'd like to think so. I really hope that doesn't come across overly confident, I'm just being honest in terms of the faith I have in this band and these boys' voices.

MICHAEL: That performance caught everybody by surprise. We got the standing ovation and then the cast came forward and we stood with them and took a bow. It was amazing. We've had so many special Collabro moments, but I think if I had to pick just one – so hard! – then performing on the *Les Misérables* stage was my most standout surreal moment to date.

JAMIE: Given our background struggling to break through in musical theatre, our battles to get a break, all the dodgy gigs, failed auditions, rejections, disappointments... for us to then perform those songs on the stage of that musical... it was just so significant, such a magical milestone. From that night on the *Les Misérables* stage was hugely symbolic for us as a band and as people.

I was on cloud nine.

In fact all of us were on cloud nine.

Then again, that's pretty much how we all feel about being in Collabro.

THE ROYAL VARIETY
PERFORMANCE

JAMIE: In late November 2014, we finally sang at the Palladium for the Royal Variety Performance, which was part of our prize for winning *Britain's Got Talent*. We had played *Sunday Night at the Palladium*, now we were there again for the Royal Variety and we will sing there on our tour, so that venue has become quite an important part of the Collabro story.

MATT: So there we are in a production meeting, sitting in the auditorium alongside Shirley Bassey, Alfie Boe, Ed Sheeran, Demi Lovato, Bette Midler, McBusted... all these incredible acts that we are big fans of. One Direction were there too.

JAMIE: We spent quite a bit of time backstage in Ed Sheeran's dressing room and Harry Styles was there too because they are good friends.

TOM: The subject of us kicking him off the Number 1 album spot never arose though, it felt like that sketch in *Fawlty Towers*, 'Don't mention the album!'

JAMIE: Elsewhere backstage Simon was chatting with us about this year's *The X Factor*, he really made an effort to chat and spend time with us, which was really nice.

TOM: When it came to our turn to perform, Simon introduced us to the audience, including mentioning our Number 1 album; he said some really nice things.

JAMIE: We were standing in silhouette at the back of the stage then as each of us sang our lines; we stepped forward into these amazing spotlights. We knew we had a job to do and we wanted to enjoy it because it was our prize for winning *Britain's Got Talent*. It's hard not to enjoy a performance like that and, besides, singing on stage is what we love to do.

RICHARD: When we bowed to the Royal Box at the end of the song it was an incredible moment, I can't wait to tell that story in years to come. I will always remember that night.

JAMIE: Some of the audience even stood up, a mini standing ovation, which was just brilliant to see.

MICHAEL: We were all really excited about meeting Prince William and the Duchess of Cambridge, Kate. William asked us what we were up to and also said something like, 'With voices like yours, I am sure you will succeed worldwide easily'. He didn't need to say anything – that was really kind.

THE ROYAL VARIETY PERFORMANCE

JAMIE: Kate looked absolutely beautiful, four months pregnant, completely glowing. She said 'Well done' and congratulated us on our success. It was Kate and William's first time at the Royal Variety too.

MICHAEL: Then I said to her, 'By the way, you look stunning.' I'm not sure you are supposed to say anything like that but she was so lovely to us and it just seemed like a nice thing to say. In return, she said we looked fantastic too. Luckily William was further along the way so he didn't hear me say his wife looked stunning!

RICHARD: Kate was then introduced to Simon and he was being a little bit mischievous, because he said to her, 'So, who do you prefer, One Direction or Collabro?' She wouldn't say, she was just really nice about both bands but he was asking her for an answer, then he smiled, laughed and said, 'I am just teasing you.' She was so lovely about everyone.

MICHAEL: Performing at the Royal Variety felt like we were closing off our *Britain's Got Talent* journey in one sense, because that was a part of our prize but was also our last involvement with the show. Now the challenge is for us to continue making Collabro a success and take Collabro global!

AFTERWORD

MICHAEL: You now know Collabro's story. It's been some journey! A key part of this fantastic, life-changing experience is the people who voted for us, who come to see us sing, who get in touch with us and support this band every day. We can never thank them enough. It is such an incredible boost to have those fans.

We all recognise how crucial those fans are because before the band kicked off, we were alone, individually struggling to make our way into this industry. We all just kept working away; there were so many low points for us all but you just have to keep trying. Never stop trying. In Collabro's case, this group had to carve out a new path. There were always going to be difficulties with that approach, but you just have to be brave and just do it.

We want to achieve so much with this band. We want to work hard, to get out there and sing to people, to try to make our mark. Having said all that, even if someone said to me tomorrow that Collabro was over and I had no money in my bank, I would still say, 'Thank you for this experience.' That is how special it has been so far.

RICHARD: I am so lucky to be able to do this; it's something truly awesome. I am so proud of what we have accomplished already and we have so much more to do. It's not just the big milestones that make your day either. Obviously winning the show, hitting Number 1 with the album or singing on a West End stage is incredible but there are other, smaller moments. Every now and then someone will message me and say, 'Richard! Your band was just a question in a pub quiz,' or I might read a comment on Facebook about someone listening to Collabro at a special moment in their life. Those little moments are really awesome; they are all a part of this amazing story. If this is your dream too, well, try to remember what I said about getting on social media. Just get something on there, post some videos, sing some songs, and get your name out there. It is up to you to keep trying. It will be worth it, trust me.

TOM: Absolutely. Also, you will find a moment – or moments – when your dream just starts to come together and then you will know you are on your way. One of those moments for us was singing 'Bring Him Home' way back at The Miller. That was a special moment and look at the amazing events that have happened to all of us since then.

All the hard graft isn't wasted either, even when you are not getting the results you want yet. Hopefully our backgrounds and struggles to make the breakthrough will help us, now that the band has taken off. When we were planning the debut headline tour, it was put to us by management that it was going to be a pretty intensive series of shows. They said, 'We are going to do three days on, one day off, okay?' I thought back to my tour of Italy, where we did six days on and one day off, so this Collabro tour sounded leisurely! Seriously though, we know there is a lot of hard work ahead... and we can't wait to get started.

MATT: We are so, so lucky that Collabro allows us to sing professionally. I don't mean in terms of success or money or acclaim. That is all great, obviously, but I mean in terms of our own personalities and lives. What we all love about performing is the fact that when you are on stage it is the one place you can just forget everything else. For that hour or two nothing else matters. If you are feeling down then performing helps so much, it is such a buzz. Whenever we have days off, I'm glad of the rest but also I get fidgety really quickly and just want to be back on stage performing again. Collabro lets us do that and for that I am hugely grateful.

Looking back on the story of Collabro so far in writing this book, it's just been the most amazing experience. I feel that we have been just so incredibly lucky. Someone put it to me recently that you make your own luck and the success of Collabro is the combined result of years of grafting. That is very true; there has been a lot of hard work and a few slices of luck along the way. We have loved every minute of it.

JAMIE: Hopefully people will read this book, follow our story and take something from that. My message to people who are struggling to find a break is to go out and find the work. Find what you want and then do it; make the opportunity happen yourself. Be proud of who you are and fight for what you want to do in life. Don't settle for second best. You only get to live once and if that means you get rejected and struggle with self-confidence issues from failed auditions, so be it. Brush yourself down and just keep going. Don't sit and wait for the next audition.

Work hard. Be patient. It will happen. If you work hard enough it will happen.

I've been lucky enough to get a break. I truly believe that people who work hard to make sure they are in the right place at the right time will eventually get there. We were five young, fresh musical theatre singers who were struggling to make it individually but who came together, with the help of some others, to form something really magical. So never, ever give up. Collabro is an overnight sensation that was a decade in the making.